Our Treasured Heritage

Our Treasured Heritage

Teaching Christian Meditation to Children

Theresa O'Callaghan Scheihing
with
Louis M. Savary

CROSSROAD • NEW YORK

1981
The Crossroad Publishing Company
575 Lexington Avenue, New York, NY 10022

Printed in the United States of America

Library of Congress Cataloging in Publication Data

Scheihing, Theresa O.
Our treasured heritage.

1. Meditation.   2.   Church year meditations.
3. Children—Religious life.   I. Savary,
Louis M.   II. Title.
BV4813.S2   248.3′4   81–7818
ISBN 0-8245-0078-4   AACR2

To my beautiful mother and grandmother,
who taught me how to meditate, I dedicate this book.

Rocking in your arms
I felt God close to me. . .

In the song of your lullaby
I heard his voice. . .

And I remember him.

Contents

Introduction

Somehow within the structure of the Christian churches we need places where people can learn to meditate in our own tradition. I mean everyday people, not just priests, ministers, monks, and religious sisters. God is calling each of us to union with him. If God is a loving parent, as Jesus revealed, then we are all called to a one-to-one relationship with God. Meditation offers the most natural way into such a relationship.

Methods for meditation have been taught throughout the centuries in certain monasteries and convents, but today's lay people, more and more frequently called to ministry and responsibility in the Church, also need sufficient spiritual resources to carry out their tasks. Practically, this means that the tradition of Christian meditation needs to be transmitted in such a way that working mothers, busy teachers, and involved fathers can learn it and pass it on to their children.

We need to train people in simple, direct ways of meditating, since most parents and teachers probably don't have the time or money to complete an extensive spiritual training program. Adults who learn some simple meditation skills can choose to set their alarms ahead twenty minutes each morning to allow for quiet, centering time in meditation, or agree to spend fifteen minutes in meditation with their children before their bedtime a few evenings each week.

But even if adults want to learn to meditate, where can they go to learn? The sad fact is that many religious leaders do not meditate, some do not even know how to meditate, and few understand the dynamics of meditation well enough to teach it. Many retreat houses invite people to spend time in prayer, yet do not teach people *how* to meditate or how to enter into contemplation. If meditation is no longer a priority among religious leaders, then others will have to take up the challenge, because people are hungry for meditation, and if they cannot find it in their Christian churches, they will search elsewhere for it. But find it they must. That's how deep and strong the call to union with God is.

Aware of these facts, as a Christian parent feeling the call to meditation, I choose to share what I have been doing and invite others to join the work of practicing and teaching meditation in whatever way they know. My exploration has been in the teaching of meditation to children—to my own two daughters and to the children I deal with at school. I haven't found many books or articles about introducing children to meditation in a Christian tradition, so most of what I share is the result of my own trials and errors, successes and failures.

In this book I hope to do a number of things. First, I would like to proclaim from the housetops that Christian meditation exists—it is alive and well and available to every man, woman, and child!—and that you and the children in your care are probably called to an ever deeper union with God to which meditation can open the door.

Second, I would like to discuss meditation and contemplation and their meaning for children. I believe that traditional forms of meditation, originally designed for monastery life, can be adapted without difficulty for present-day use by adults and children. I want to stress again and again the immense value of meditation to you and your children in contemporary society. Meditation is not only timely for us; it is a crucial need at a critical moment in history.

Third, I want to offer many practical suggestions for introducing your children to this treasured Christian tradition, so that once you understand what meditation is, you will have ways of showing your children (and yourselves) how to build a loving, intimate relationship with God. I have included a list of questions most frequently asked by parents and teachers about children and meditation. I try to answer them in Part II of this book.

Fourth, I offer outlines for dozens of meditations for children based on special times in the Church's liturgical year— Advent, Christmas, Lent, Easter, Ascension, Pentecost, and others. The meditations are presented in sets of five, so that teachers who wish to use a meditation each weekday may do so. All these units have been used successfully by parents and teachers. You can use my meditational model (which is taken from Ignatius Loyola's *Spiritual Exercises*) to create your own meditations.

You may also discover your children creating their own meditational and centering material. When that day happens, rejoice, for you will know that you have handed on the spark of meditation to your children and brought them to a place where they can, if necessary, continue alone in working at their unique relationship with God.

My ultimate desire is to invite as many people as possible into a deeper, loving, personal relationship with God. Where better to begin than with children, to whom, Jesus assures us, belongs the kingdom of God? To have made your children fully conscious, through direct experience in meditation, of their relationship to God and to the kingdom is to have handed on to them our precious Christian heritage as sons and daughters of God.

This book overflows with the experience and expertise of the many who have shaped my approach to meditation. First of all, I would like to thank Louis M. Savary, who introduced me to Ignatian meditation with music, encouraged me to write this book, and assisted in its editorial development. Second, I am deeply grateful to Monsignor Gerard Fahey, Pastor of St. Eugene's Cathedral, for his visionary insight into the value of meditative prayer for children. His support and enthusiasm enabled me to pursue the exploration and development of the meditation experiences presented in this book. Third, I would like to thank my friend and colleague, Sister JoAnn Consiglieri, with whom I shared the challenge of creating daily meditations for children at St. Eugene's Elementary School. I am especially grateful to those children, parents, and priests at St. Eugene's who were willing to explore the possibilities of teaching meditation in classroom situations and for remaining trustfully supportive of me during failures, as well as successes. For me it was an exhilarating experience of the Holy Spirit at work among us. Finally, and this is the most important acknowledgment of all, I want to thank my two loving daughters, Maria and Angela, for sharing many of their contemplative moments with me, teaching me how deeply God relates to children, and never ceasing to call me—even during difficult times—to my responsibility of companioning them in prayer.

Theresa O'Callaghan Scheihing

Part One

MEDITATION AND CENTERING: WHAT DO THEY MEAN TO CHILDREN?

CHAPTER 1

What are Meditation and Centering for Children?

MEDITATION AND PRAYER

Meditation is a special way of praying. Prayer in general, traditionally defined as lifting the mind and the heart to God, involves a focusing on or paying attention to God and the things of God. In prayer, people often recite well-known verses or spontaneously speak words of praise, gratitude, petition, or sorrow to God. This kind of praying, basically one-directional, flows from humans to God.

Meditation is a two-way experience. It involves talking to God and listening to God, intending to build a one-to-one relationship with God characterized by personal, intimate, loving exchange. It is the mutual talking and listening in meditation that bring about a union between the believer and God.

On the emotional level, meditation evokes personal, secure, close feelings in children. When children enjoy an intimate talk with God, they can sense something happening between their hearts and God's heart.

CENTERING AND PRAYER

Centering is also a special way of praying. It involves a relaxation and quietness that allows you, first, to be in touch with your own center (or heart) and, second, to be aware that God is actively and lovingly present to you there.

To help children get centered, I sometimes suggest that they imagine Jesus holding their hands and walking with them on a pathway that leads to their centers. I might say, "Your center is the place in you where you and God can be together in a very special way, and Jesus will lead you there. It is the place where you feel most comfortable and safe in all the world. It is a place within you where you feel closest to yourself and closest to God."

I realize that a person's center, like their soul or spirit, is not precisely a "place," yet most people doing centering prayer seem to associate their centers with a place in their bodies. Some feel centered in their heads, others near their lower intestines; most seem to locate their center in the area around their physical hearts. For this reason, I often use the terms "center" and "heart" interchangeably.

When you are in touch with your center or heart and totally present to it, we say that you are *centered*. When you are also in touch with God's presence within you and are resting in that presence, you are doing *centering prayer*. There is nothing subtle or complicated about it. It is a very simple yet powerful way of uniting with God. Centering usually does not involve thinking actively except by being attentive and aware.

Children grasp the idea of centering very easily. With practice they can learn to get centered on God in just a very few minutes.

When I first introduce children to a centering experience, I usually say something like this: "You are going to go deeply within yourself, to a place you have been to before, a place you may not have recognized or named before, but it won't be completely new. The closer you get to it, the more you'll recognize you have been there before. Your center has a special feeling connected to it. It's a quiet feeling and a sacred feeling, and it's also very exciting. It's the feeling of being alive and it's a wonderful feeling."

My daughter Maria told me once, "Being at your center feels like being held and rocked by someone who loves you with all their heart."

While centering by itself is a very legitimate and ancient Christian prayer form,* I present it in this book mainly as an important stepping stone to meditation.

SILENCE, OPENNESS, AND LISTENING

Three things that help prepare for union with God are silence, openness, and listening. In meditation and centering a child learns to *listen*, not with ordinary ears, but with "inner ears." The *silence* of meditation begins with external silence, but includes internal silence of mind. Some children describe inner silence as the mind going blank, waiting for a picture to appear and focus. The *openness* that happens during meditation and centering is also a quality of the heart. When the mind goes blank, the heart opens to an inner flow and something gets written on the blank mind. Something connects between the heart and mind which involves both feelings and imagination. The connection seems to happen when people don't force it to happen, when they remain receptive without trying to control the experience.

When you begin thinking about Jesus on the level of feeling, your imagination gets carried into the experience and you begin asking all kinds of questions about Jesus: What does he look like? What is he doing? What is he feeling right now? But most of all, you know you want to be with him. You can feel his attraction in your heart. You can feel yourself

* See, for example, *Centering Prayer: A New Approach to Meditation* (New York: Doubleday, 1980), written by M. Basil Pennington, a Trappist monk.

saying, "I want to be with you. There is no place else I'd rather be now than with you."

When children are preparing to meditate like this, I usually recommend a prayer of trust, because children experience meditation as a stepping into sacred ground, new territory, the unknown. To encourage their trust I might say, "It will be like taking Jesus' hand and tiptoeing. He leads you to a new place. You don't know where you're going, but as you go there it feels very familiar, as if you've been there before. The more often you go into the world of meditation and the more firmly you hold onto Jesus' hand, the more surely you'll know you've been there before."

The excitement of meditation for children begins with the emotions. They realize with delight and surprise that they don't have to do anything to get there, even though it's a new place. As soon as they get on the road, they recognize that what they're feeling is not new at all. And they're not afraid of it.

THE RHYTHM OF MEDITATION

Besides the feeling of having been there before, there is another important experience encountered by children in meditation. It involves the rhythm or step which takes you into the experience. The rhythmic motion of meditation feels like being rocked and held very closely. Once you know that feeling, you will never forget it, just as you can never forget how it felt to be held closely and rocked in your grandmother's arms.

Once children experience this closeness and intimacy in meditation, they want to meditate. They are ready to jump into it and enjoy it. Once they jump in, there is nothing to do except to stay there, since meditation is a way of *being*, not doing.

One evening, while I was meditating with my nine-year-old daughter, I asked her to describe how it felt. We began a stream of consciousness exchange which went something like this:

"It feels good, because I feel good inside. I feel peaceful and happy."

"What else does it feel like?" I asked.

"It feels like me and something else, like a coming-together feeling. I'm not afraid to feel this. Something else is filling me and I like it and I want to feel it more. I don't have to do anything. It just fills me. But I don't know what it is that fills me."

"Could it be God?" I ask.

"Maybe," was her reply.

"What does it feel like?" I ask again.

"It makes me want to do more. It's overflowing inside me."

"What is there?"

"I don't know everything that's there. I can tell you some of the things. There's a joy feeling and a feeling that I may want to cry. And there's another thing I can't name, a thing that happens. The thing I don't have a word for happens when I hold onto the hand. And when I let go, it stops."

"What is it?" I ask.

"I don't know," she replies.

"Who is it?" I ask again.

"I don't know, but when I trust it, it fills me."

"It? What is it?" I gently insist.

"Something that keeps growing and keeps me growing inside. It's like growing into a center. We're connected. I know that feeling. I've felt it before."

"What is the feeling?" I ask.

"It's safe and it's rocking and then it happens."

"What happens?" I ask.

"Nothing happens. Silence happens."

"What's happening in the silence?" I ask.

"Everything is happening there. It's a fullness. It's a touching. God is touching me."

"How do you know it's God?" I ask.

"He touches me from inside, gently."

"With fingers?" I ask for clarification.

"Not really. It's like a rippling. I hold onto him and he holds onto me. It's like we're hugging."

"How can you hug somebody you can't see?"

"You can feel it. I feel the hug someplace inside me."

"Where?" I ask.

"I don't know where, but I know I feel it. It's a growing feeling."

How exciting it is to feel the mystery present when a child meditates! What does a parent do in the face of this awesome divine energy?

SOMETHING DIFFERENT

I have taken the time to help my children to learn to meditate. This example of dialogue with my nine-year-old shows that children are capable of deep meditational experiences. What did I do to foster this almost mystical sense in her? It seems to me, as I look back, that I did next to nothing. But when someone questioned me about it, I began to recall details of our relationship during prayer time that might be important. Like many mothers, I presumed that every other mother probably did what I did when I took the children to bed and told them to say their prayers. I have since discovered my assumption was not true. I did do some things differently. That is why I wish to share my experience with you, the experience that led me to introducing children to deeper forms of prayer.

CHAPTER 2

The Atmosphere of Prayer

CENTERING: FINDING A SILENT AND PRIVATE PLACE

One thing I'm really sure of is that there is a need in the heart of every person—child, working person, college professor, bishop—to experience the silence and privacy, the one-to-one relationship with God that the prayerful monk in the monastery experiences during meditation. Everyone needs to find and care for this silent and private place in his or her heart. To find that place and to act from it is to be centered. Some artists find it when they are practicing their craft, other people find it in their relationship with nature, still others find their way to it through the reflective corridors of the mind. Without knowing your way to this kind of silence and privacy, without knowing how to get centered, you cannot go far in meditation.

No matter how many books on centering and meditation you study, they cannot give your heart silence and privacy. It is an experience we struggle to discover for ourselves or, luckily, we are led into it by someone who loves us enough to take the time to show us the way, someone who is willing to hold our hands and lead us into the silence until God's hand takes over.

MEDITATION AND CONTEMPLATION

People sometimes ask me to tell them what higher prayer means, to define, for example, the difference between meditation and contemplation. For me, meditation and contemplation are closely related. Meditation is often a preparation for contemplation. I view meditation as the more organized part of relating to God, the step-by-step part we can control to some degree. Contemplation, on the other hand, is something that happens in response to God's invitation to a heart-to-heart relationship.

Contemplation, this one-to-one union with God, is meant to be very natural to us, and at the same time an exceptional experience, because it is a gift which invites us to enter into the Center of life and love. While you can prepare for meditation, the contemplative experience, like any spontaneous and deep encounter with another, either happens or doesn't. It is beyond our control.

NATURAL CONTEMPLATIVES

What continues to overwhelm me as I prepare children for meditation and contemplation is the undeniable fact that many of them are already familiar with the contemplative experience. I need do very little to prepare them, except make them aware that they are already practicing contemplation.

What is intriguing to me is that many, if not most, children move in and out of contemplation naturally and spontaneously. This fact clearly contradicts what many of the manuals on higher states of prayer assert, that the contemplative experience is scarce and rare. On the contrary, what I see while teaching prayer to children is that contemplation is natural to them. Once invited into the silence and privacy of their own inner core, they simply come aglow. Theirs is a knowledge of contemplation that comes from within, a knowing that was present long before I ever met them.

I cannot stress this enough. It does not take any technical knowledge to engage in contemplation. There are no course requirements, no necessary books to read. Everyone, especially every child, has an innate aptitude for contemplation.

A CONTEMPLATIVE ENVIRONMENT

Usually I find that all I need to do to stimulate a contemplative moment in children is to create an appropriate environment. Once the child feels relaxed, once his or her imagination is open and flowing, and once his or her heart can trust that it is being held and led by God, then, with no expectation of what to do or how to do it, contemplation happens.

Sometimes, however, a child's imagination does not flow, the movement does not happen, even when the child appears relaxed and trusting. When a situation like this happens, I tend to look for some anger or fear that is blocking the flow. For example, my daughter and I were sitting next to each other on her bed one Saturday afternoon after she had washed her hair and was drying it. She saw me preparing some meditations for next week's religion classes and asked if she could do one. Agreeing, I told her about Jesus' parable of the mustard seed and how she was like that seed. She closed her eyes and snuggled up to me, and my natural response was to hold her. She seemed relaxed and trusting but nothing was flowing in her imagination. I suspected that she might be blocked by anger. So, holding her close, I asked very gently, "Is there someone who has hurt you?" I felt a twinge of movement in her. I evidently had touched the thing that was blocking the flow. "Would you like to say something about it?" I asked. "Can you forgive someone?"

Without saying a word, she reached out and touched my arm, knowing instinctively that she could let go of her anger. There was a way to let go of it, there was a way to open the flow again, a nonreflective way. She had found it and was then able to be present to the Presence again, to be in the contemplative state. For her, and for most children, being able to reach deeper prayer states has something to do with trust. Here, I was able to help my daughter create an atmosphere of closeness, a safe place, within which she was no longer afraid to let her anger out and allow forgiveness in.

I did not know who had hurt her or at whom her anger might have been directed. Nor did I probe to find out. I respect her right to privacy in such matters. Usually she tells me about it, but this time she didn't. (Actually, she did later.) What she needed from me at the moment was simply the assurance that she was in a safe emotional environment.

Contemplation for children—and adults, too—happens in an atmosphere of closeness and trust. Parents and teachers can provide such an atmosphere, sometimes verbally. But, more often, gentle words need to be reinforced by holding, touching, eye contact, and an undistracted presence to the child.

Music and Contemplation

I frequently use background music to facilitate a meditation or contemplation. For me, appropriate music can symbolize the contemplative space and reflect it. Music's healing power, which seems to come from its rhythm and melody, symbolizes something familiar, consistent, trustworthy. Its rhythm holds you in its arms and gently rocks you, reassuring you that you are safe there; its melody seems to take you by the hand and lead you toward the feelings inside. You may never have heard the melody before, but yet somehow you *have* heard it, because every melody in its own unique way says, "God, God, God," or announces some facet of God's life, such as Jesus, hope, joy, love, faith, or deepening. As a melody starts to move in you, it releases the flow of certain "God feelings"—love, peace, joy, forgiveness—whatever feelings it knows how to release. A melody facilitates contact with the "God feelings" that are ready to happen inside you.

In meditation, music acts like a stream flowing through and around things. God is like the flow. Music gets you into the "God flow" and allows you to experience that flow, which is always the same, yet always different, always unknown, yet always familiar.

I played music for some meditating six-year-olds in class, told them to imagine themselves on a riverbank building a raft, and encouraged them to feel the excitement of getting on the raft and trusting it to take them on a journey downriver. The music activated their feelings more quickly than I could have done with mere words.

As soon as they could trust the music, it carried them into the flow. For the next few minutes I left them in the hands of the music, letting it guide their imaginary voyage into the "God flow." Afterwards, one child reported having seen people dancing on the riverbank, had entered the dancing, and discovered that the dancers and the dancing entered into him. He was entering into the joy of God.

As the melody shifted, one child saw giant boulders in the river just ahead and the rafting children wondered how they were going to get through. The music helped them maneuver their way. And without expressing it in words, this child knew how God's spirit can make its way through the obstacles in a human heart. The child had received a gift of God's wisdom!

Music is so essentially helpful that I don't know how else to nurture such depth and intensity of contemplation in children. Without music, I can help children into contemplation, but their experience never seems to have the dramatic flow that it has *with* music. Appropriate music keeps the flow going. It carries you over, around, and through things that would otherwise stop the flow. It goes fast when you need to push forward, it slows down when you need to be reflective.

Almost magically, music, when you trust it, takes you where you need to go.

In meditation and contemplation for children, the imagination is very important. When images bubble up in their imaginations during meditation, some children don't know what to do. The most helpful thing for them to do is to enter into the flow of the images. Some people have a sense of what an image means; others need help understanding it. Don't worry about meaning at first; simply help children to get into the flow of music and images.

Some children will need to have your permission to get into the flow, fearing what they are doing might be wrong. Other children intuitively know they have permission; they carry permission within themselves to enter the flow and be guided by it. Such children are rare, since so many of us have been told that imagination has nothing to do with prayer, that its use is mere daydreaming, a worthless pastime. Most children need an adult to guide them toward the flow of images and give them permission to enter it.

My experience with children is this: their approach is very different from that of adults. Adults usually have a fixed idea of the way things *should be;* even their spontaneous experiences are often mentally programmed. In contrast, children are open to seeing things exactly as they are, so their spontaneous experiences, such as the flow of images, are *really* spontaneous.

Because of this difference, adults introducing children to meditation need to be wary of the adult tendency to steer a child's experience rather than guide it, to direct it rather than facilitate it. Parents who feel a strong moral obligation to tell their children what they should visualize tend to hinder contemplation.

When adults do not try to direct their children's minds,

those minds become a revelation to parents and teachers. For example, one evening I was meditating with my daughters and, as usual, I asked them to tell me what was happneing inside them. My younger daughter, Angela, began, "Mom, it's like . . ." and she stopped. And without opening her eyes or letting go of my hand, she asked, "Mom, what's the matter?"

"Nothing," I replied, deciding that I did not wish to share my problems with my children.

"Why are you sad?" she asked, and then continued, offering the consoling wisdom that was spontaneously flowing through her. "Don't you know that Jesus loves you? It's not going to be heavy all the time."

How had she intuited my sadness? How did she know the words that would penetrate my heart? I had no doubt that my six-year-old was in touch with God.

A TIME FOR LEARNING

I find in my children a tremendous desire to learn things about their own spiritual natures. At night, when I tuck the children in, I make a point of spending some time with each of them and of being especially sensitive to their feelings at that time. They will usually signal their need to learn something with phrases like, "I don't feel so good," or "Stay with me longer."

Then I might ask, "What's the matter?"

"My tummy hurts."

After checking to see that she is not physically ill, I ask "Why?"

"I don't know why, but I just don't feel good."

"Do you want to feel better?" I ask, inviting her commitment to the learning and healing process.

"Yes," comes the invariable reply.

"Okay. When did you start getting the stomach ache? An hour ago? Do you remember when it began?"

"When I was playing at recess."

"What did it feel like then?"

"I just wanted to cry."

"Are you crying inside now?"

"Yes."

"Something is hurting you." I say it clearly, so that both of us are sure what the learning task will be. And I add, "Do you want to go to sleep with the hurting?"

"No," she replies. "I'm afraid I'm going to wake up in the middle of the night and it will be scary."

"What can I do to help?" I ask, trusting that her inner self will tell me what I can do to help the process of healing.

"Hold me and sing me a song," she says. Her request is not a ruse to get me to stay with her a while. She knows that she can best become relaxed, open, and trusting when I hold her and sing. She knows what she needs and I trust her request.

"What song?" I ask, holding her.

"Too-ra-loo-ra, or make up a song that makes the pain go away. Sing the one that Nanny used to sing."

So I sing it, holding her.

"Do you want to let your pain go?" I ask after the song. She nods. "You want to get into dreamland, but you need a ticket. The ticket," I stress, "is to want to get there and to want to let go of your pain." She nods again, knowing the truth of what I have just said.

"How big is the pain?" I ask. "Where is it located in your body?" I have never met a child who can't tell me where the pain is. She points to her stomach.

"Are you afraid of it?" I ask. When she nods yes, I suggest, "If I go inside with you, will you be afraid?"

"No," she says, so in our imaginations we go inside together to look at the fear.

"Look at it," I say. "Talk to it. Tell it, 'Okay, fear, I'm coming in. I'm with my mom and I'm not afraid of you anymore. And I don't want you inside of me.' "

I allow her time to confront the fear.

"What does your fear look like?" I ask her.

"Awful and ugly," she replies.

"How big is it? Big as a soccer ball? Or a grapefruit?" By now I can tell that she is deeply in a meditative state and I introduce her once again to Jesus. I might say something like, "Honey, I can't take your pain away. I would if I could. But Jesus can. He had a way of healing people who hurt the way you do. There are stories in a book about Jesus called the New Testament that tell about people who were really hurting inside, like you. Jesus was able to do something to get rid of these feelings, and their pain started going away. Jesus can show you how to take your fear and pain away, if you let him."

PARENTS AS GUIDES

Once the child is in touch with Jesus, my work of guidance is usually over. Parents may feel they should be doing something at this point to guide the child's thoughts. There is no need for this. The child is in contemplation. God has taken over the process. God, or Jesus, alone takes the child on an inner journey—a journey of learning and healing.

My task has been to lead the child to this point of departure, from a place of fear to a place that, though still unknown, was a safe place. To do my task, I needed to hold my child, sing to her, weave a story, and provide a place of safety, so she could let go and entrust herself to Jesus in contemplation.

CONTEMPLATION AND SLEEP

For many children, it is natural to move from the contemplative state to peaceful sleep. Therefore, a good meditation time for them is the time just before sleep. I usually begin by tucking each child into bed. Often I sit on their beds and hold them, perhaps even rocking them or stroking them and humming a melody. I then ask them if they would like to go into dreamland with Jesus. I remind them that the only way to go into dreamland is by really wanting to go there, and the only things that keep you out of dreamland are fear and anger. I might ask them if they have any fear or anger to let go of. If not, I ask them to close their eyes and picture Jesus in their minds. Then I suggest thinking of a word or phrase, like "Jesus, I love you," and saying it again and again. "Everytime you say it," I assure them, "you go deeper and deeper into dreamland."

When, at bedtime, children have more time for meditating and you can afford to be *fully* present to them, you may invite them to continue weaving a story about Jesus you begin for them. Because a child's mind is ripe, open, and receptive, they love to follow the inner drama of such imagery. When you are not sure where to begin, simply ask the child, "What are you thinking about?" or "Where would you like to go with Jesus in dreamland tonight?" Usually they will offer you an image with which to begin the meditation. Use it as a gateway to lead them where their spirits need to go. Let them talk to Jesus about it.

CONNECTING WITH GOD AND JESUS

Some adults wonder: Can you meditate on things other than Scripture? If you do, is it really prayer?

My reply to this is: If you are talking to Jesus or listening to him, then any topic is meditation, any topic is prayer.

The important thing in meditation is *listening.* You need to learn to listen in an unusual way, for Jesus does not communicate with words but with inner movements and imagery. For example, when you are happily excited, that good feeling of yours connects you with the good feelings of Jesus. Or maybe the image of a butterfly or a blossom connects you with Jesus' joy. How the connection is made doesn't really matter.

What matters is that your center connects with Jesus' center. Anything that is not a destructive feeling (like anger) or not an isolating feeling (like fear) offers a way of connecting with God. For some, a pillow, a teddy bear, a living pet can awaken feelings of loving and being loved. This may be their way into contemplation. My daughter Maria puts her grandmother's blanket around her at night, whether it's hot or cold. For her the blanket has life and power; it provides inner security and connects her with God. When she's wrapped in her blanket, it can symbolize God. When she tells me she can go to sleep and keep God wrapped around her all night long, I know she has found a way to enter a contemplative state and to remain in it.

Colors of the rainbow are another effective way for helping children connect affectively with God. I usually suggest that each color represents a different "God feeling"—love, friendship, helping, joy, forgiveness, etc. The different colors stand for different feelings Jesus can give you, or for the different ways you can feel toward Jesus. Thus, each color of the rainbow offers an invitation to contemplation.

CHAPTER 3

Christian Traditions of Prayer

Unfamiliarity with Meditation and Centering

Children are such natural contemplatives that they are surprised to discover that their parents may be unfamiliar with meditation and centering. "Why weren't my parents taught to meditate like we were?" is a question many of my students ask me. "When I tell my mother how we get centered and meditate in class, she says she never learned how to do it."

When people ask me what it takes to learn to meditate, I usually reply, "If you can talk, listen and be silent, you can learn to meditate. And, of course, you need to want to know and love God."

Sometimes parents mistakenly feel that centering and meditation are just fads or esoteric rituals started by an eastern guru in California, and they ask me why they weren't taught to do such things in school. I usually reply they had probably been taught to meditate long before they began school. Then I explain the way I learned to meditate. "My grandmother and my mother often meditated with me, except they didn't call it meditation. They held me on their laps and rocked me, they made me feel quiet and safe, and they showed me how to love Jesus. There were no formulas.

32

Nobody called it meditation, but it was essentially the same process I'm teaching your children."

The essence of meditation is a relationship with God, which generates a feeling of being related heart-to-heart to him. I knew that feeling when my grandmother rocked me on her lap and sang "too-ra-loo-ra," and I knew it when my mother sat beside me in bed and said, "Close your eyes, honey. Jesus loves you. He's here." In that moment I felt safe and close to him. That was a contemplative moment. It's the same feeling the saints and mystics describe. If you ever felt that feeling of being safe and close to God, then you have experienced contemplation; you know what I am teaching your children. And you can teach it to them too, just the way I do—if you're not already doing it.

Just be sure to tell your children that they are meditating, that when they feel close to Jesus they are practicing contemplation. Tell them they can keep meditating and contemplating God this way for the rest of their lives.

A Christian Birthright

It saddens me when parents ask me if I am encouraging some kind of Eastern religious cult when I teach their children to meditate. How unfortunate it is that some Christian adults have never been in touch with the meditative and mystic traditions of the Christian Church! How sad that there are so few places in the Church today where adults can learn centering and meditation. How sad that a Church that proclaims loving, intimate union with God fails to offer ways for believers to experience this contemplative union.

"No," I tell the sometimes frightened parents, "I'm not leading your children into a weird cult. I'm introducing your children into their birthright as Christians. I'm offering them a way to begin experiencing the intimate union with God their hearts cry out for. Help them by supporting me and reinforcing what I say to them. I am aware no one taught you centering and meditation when you were young. But please don't deprive your children of this tremendous privilege. I hope that we adults will be the last generation to say we were never taught to meditate by our Church."

I know of many young men and women in search of deep meditative experience who have felt it necessary to go elsewhere to find spiritual wisdom because their own community of faith had not provided a way to enter this deeper kind of experience. I am grateful I did find someone in my own church who showed me how to meditate in practical ways so it could—and did—become a part of my life. I believe that meditation should be taught in our churches, and I believe that it is beginning to be taught. I have taught it to my own children and to the children I have in class. At times, these children's parents, who have known only vocal prayer and liturgical prayer, are confused about, or fearful of, what I am teaching their children. I try to assure these adults the prayer they were taught is good and beautiful, but that there are also other good and beautiful experiences of prayer called centering, meditation, and contemplation.

DIFFERENT STYLES OF PRAYING

While the churches have emphasized vocal and liturgical styles of prayer which focus on *exterior* things, such as books, public rituals, songs, gestures, and recited formulas, the call to meditation is a call to *interior* things. When children and adults allow themselves to grow silent inside, they will feel the need for this interior experience. Meditation is not a fad, but an expression of the cry of the spirit for direct contact with the living God. It is at the heart of our Christian faith and experience.

The objective of meditation is, very simply, a personal, intimate, loving relationship to the living Christ. While the goal of liturgical and public prayer is to join a believing community to God, meditation's intent is to focus on the personal relationship of an individual believer and God. Neither kind of prayer is wrong; one is not better than the other. Both are treasured parts of our Christian heritage. We need not eliminate either public and external styles of prayer or interior ones. We should practice and nurture them all. Even though this book is devoted to the practice of meditation, I do not wish in any way to discourage or denigrate other ways of finding God.

It may be helpful at this point to look at some traditional and popular prayer forms and ask how meditation relates to them. All Christian traditions encourage congregational worship, as well as reflection on the Bible and other spiritual writings. The Catholic Church offers believers other devotional prayer forms, such as the Rosary and the Way of the Cross, which may be practiced either congregationally or privately.

When I ask Catholic parents, "Do you know what the Rosary is and how to say it?" or "Do you know how to make the Way of the Cross?" I have never found anyone who isn't familiar with both. Yet when I ask the same people, "Do you know what meditation is and how to meditate?" almost always they say no. There is a widespread lack of knowledge about meditation, and the fear, anger and mistrust people have about it stems from the fact that to them, meditation is a mysterious unknown. People tend naturally to fear and mistrust the unknown. How I long for the ways of meditation to become everyday knowledge in the churches!

What I want to stress is that meditation is not in competition with devotions like the Rosary, the Way of the Cross, the Bible, and other spiritual reading. All these forms of prayer are complementary. They all qualify as prayer because each of them is intended to elevate the mind and heart to God, to evoke expressions of love, and to encourage a relationship with God. Each one manifests God and one's relationship to God in a different way. Some are active and externalized, some are quieter and more intimate. Each style of praying leads a different part of us to God; together they lead the whole of who we are to God.

SOME CONTRASTING STYLES OF PRAYER

Some prayers require us to do something physically, such as hold a book, recite certain words, take a certain posture, or sing a hymn. Other prayers, like meditation and spiritual reading, when you let the words speak to your heart, focus more on *being*. In these prayers, it is the quality of presence and the desire for relationship that are more important. Some prayers follow a fixed procedure or ritual. Meditation has no order that must be observed. Some popular prayers are intended to put you in touch with a community of believers and God. Meditation puts you in touch with yourself and God. Some prayers involve only speaking to God. Meditation focuses also on listening to God.

In prayer forms such as the Rosary, the Way of the Cross, the eucharistic celebration, and other liturgical services, established formulas and structures provide a sense of the known, the familiar, and the predictable. In contrast, meditation may cause apprehension for some, precisely because it involves the unknown and the unpredictable. In meditation you create an atmosphere of silence, openness, and receptivity to God, having no sense of what may happen, or, rather, leaving what happens up to God. While structured prayers usually have something going on at all times, meditation may involve periods of emptiness and void when nothing seems to be happening. The challenge here is to remain open and receptive through the empty times, continuing to yearn for a more intimate relationship with God. Even children know periods of emptiness in their meditative life, as well as mysterious times when God comes to take them by the hand into unknown places. At times such as these, parents and teachers can help children bridge these new places by evoking appropriate imagery from a child's imagination.

THE VALUE OF IMAGINATION

Perhaps the most important characteristic that makes meditation different from other prayer styles, especially for children, is its use of imagination. For children, playing and praying (meditatively) are similar, first, because both play and meditation often have an imaginative component, second, because in both there is nothing to work at and, third, because both are experienced as gifts.

Some parents and teachers are puzzled when I associate prayer and imagination. For them, imagination seems to be of little value; it leads to daydreaming, they believe, and away from the praying that needs to be done. "Stop daydreaming and pay attention," was the all-too-familiar command of school teachers when I was growing up. How I wish I had known then what I know now and had had the courage to say to them, "Don't you realize that all the creativity of the world comes through imagination? It's imagination that reaches out into the future and invites us to grow. Don't you realize that imagination is the only human power that can unify a person's body, mind, emotions, and spirit? Imagination is a bridge to God. Don't you realize that we need imagination to unify our lives in terms of their meaning and purpose? Jesus counts on our imaginations to help us grasp the meaning of God's kingdom every time he uses a metaphor or tells a parable. What else but imagination could transform Jesus' images of yeast, mustard seeds, pearls, coins, storehouses, fields, and fishnets into spiritual awareness and the energy of faith? Don't you realize that imagination in a believer provides the very eyes of faith?

To tell a child, "Stop using your imagination" is to stifle a most precious part of their humanness. To block imagination in a child is to close gateways to prayer, faith, creativity, hope, and love—qualities in which our Christian religion calls us to excel. Without imagination, prayer is too often reduced to empty ritual, faith to duty, creativity to conformity, hope to fear, and love to law.

Let's face it, we have suppressed the imagination for generations. We could spend pages of print and huge amounts of energy investigating who's to blame for this sad situation. But I'd rather spend that energy and those words to reawaken capacities of imagination in our children and in ourselves. Very few of us grew up without having our imaginative abilities wounded. We need to reverse the negative assessment of imagination and to heal its wounds, using our imaginations more and more. Being able to pattern the imagination creatively and effectively is an acquired skill. It is like learning how to play basketball or a guitar. Imagination needs to be practiced habitually and with discipline. The more developed the imagination, the more valuable it becomes in meditation. The more imaginative awareness is focused, the more awareness of God can grow.

THE GROWING ACCEPTANCE OF MEDITATION

The use of informal and meditative prayer is sprouting up in many places. People feel freer than ever today to engage in spontaneous prayers before meals, before meetings, and at school. While many still recite the standard formula of grace before meals, many others create spontaneous blessings. While many meetings still begin with a perfunctory recitation of the Lord's Prayer, there are some leaders who begin with a silent prayer calling people to be aware of God's presence in their midst or who speak words like, "Whatever happens tonight, let's allow the Holy Spirit to move in us." Still others read a few verses from the Bible and ask the people present to reflect and comment on them.

In recent years we have seen a growing interest in meditation, focusing, relaxing and centering, as witnessed by many books and articles. If the Maharishi did nothing else, he did make us conscious of meditation, and perhaps inspired us to reexplore our own Western traditions of prayer and meditation.

A meditative attitude is encouraged in the liturgy. At the Roman Catholic Mass, the congregation is advised to reflect on the biblical readings, to pause and meditate on the gospel, and to spend a few contemplative minutes after Communion.

I recall, too, some meditative moments in an Advent candlelight service we had at our church; it turned out to be truly a time of silence, quieting the outer senses to let the inner senses come alive. Like a meditation, the service led us into the unknown. A baby was to be born, that we knew. "But who knows what its face will look like?," the celebrant asked. "Can you see its face?" Suddenly, with this question, Christmas preparations were transformed into a new adventure. To fully respond to the question, "Can you see its face?" the children had to be at peace with themselves and to be able to sit quietly and relax. Once they reached a peaceful and relaxed place inside, they needed only to receive the question to begin releasing its energy in their spirits. At a moment like this, God activates each child, and each one responds uniquely, picturing the baby in his or her own way. Perhaps for some the baby's face does not appear, but even these will often report feeling the presence of God within them.

As you read the New Testament, notice how everything Jesus said about his relationship to his Father implies this same kind of meditational intimacy. When Jesus prayed in the mountains or in the garden, he showed that he was aware of a meditative way to God through speaking and listening, being receptive to whatever happens. In this, Jesus is the model for the meditative tradition we pass on to our children.

Children meditating are called upon to use their minds and to explore their feelings in ways they seldom do at home or in school. In meditation, after they are presented with a thought, a story, a symbol, something upon which to focus, they are then given permission to go with it, create with it, fly with it. And when children allow a symbol or image to flow, it often goes beyond what they thought or expected. That's when meditation gets exciting, when you soar with it and it takes you beyond limits and formulas.

Children in school and at home know what they *should* do, they know what the limits are and how to follow rules. They know how to carry out orders and fulfill expectations. The responses of daily life are well-known and safe because they have boundaries and controls.

But in their imaginations children can let go of limits and allow to happen there what is beyond the realm of "shoulds." This is the way of meditation and contemplation. Its objective is not to lose control of life but to find meaning and directions for life in a way that does not require orders and expectations.

This new-found freedom often feels so good you want to keep doing it over and over again. It's like wanting to be with a good friend more and more often. Peaceful feelings are the keynotes of meditation, not anxiety, fear, or guilt. In fact, meditation sometimes feels so good you may resist returning to ordinary consciousness; it's like really enjoying yourself during recess and not wanting to return to the classroom. Much of the mental activity of meditation is carried on by the intuitive, metaphoric, and affective functions of the brain or mind; the consequent flowing and expanding feelings are quite natural.

The mind operates in two basic styles. One style, usually associated with the brain's left hemisphere, favors rational, analytical, linear, verbal, and conceptual ways of thinking.

This style receives much emphasis in school and business. The second style, usually referred to as right hemisphere activity, involves nonrational, intuitive, affective, nonverbal, metaphoric, and creative ways of thinking. Such activity is important in meditation, in which we invite children's minds to wonder, imagine, dream, discover, and explore the dimensions of awe, mystery, and God.

The body also plays an important role when children meditate. Here again, adults tend to enter meditation with preconceived notions of what the body should be doing or how the body should respond, while children tend not to have such expectations. For them the objective is simply to let go physically, to let their bodies go with the meditation as naturally as they let their mind go with it. Children meditating will often freely move their hands, arms, feet, heads, and their entire bodies.

During a meditation on the pearl of great price, I asked my daughter Angela to go inside the oyster shell to see what the pearl looked like. Her facial responses told me she was struggling to get inside the shell, or at least to look inside. Then spontaneously she shaped her hands into a heart. She was telling me she could see a heartshaped pearl.

If you let your body and mind get into the flow, meditation is an exciting and spontaneous joy. It is a natural state of being for human beings. For my children, asking them if they'd like to meditate is like asking them if they'd like an ice cream cone. And how eager they are to share, to tell me what they experience in meditation!

WHAT ADULTS CAN DO

It is important to say again that I am usually present when my own children or my students meditate. Being present helps build a deep bond between adults and children. The quality of adult presence is important, so whether you have five minutes or twenty minutes to spare, let your children know that you have nothing more important to do for that period than to be with them. Also, create an atmosphere with few distractions, turning off the stereo, closing the door, perhaps even taking the telephone off the hook. Since the time just before sleep is naturally the quietest one for my family, it has provided the best opportunity for a one-to-one relationship between my children and me.

As a prelude to meditation at bedtime, you might tell your children that you love them and that they can let all the cares and worries of the day disappear. (Let your own cares and worries go for the moment, too.) Show them nonverbally, too, that you love them and that they can let go, perhaps by holding them or sitting nearby. Remember, nobody can begin meditating instantly; you and your child will need to relax and build up a bond of trust between you before you begin. For meditating with children the prerequisites are, first, that they know you will remain present to them and, second, that it's safe for them to let go, to enter the flow within the security of your full presence.

Helping Children into Meditation

One way to begin meditative movement in a child is to ask, "How do you feel?" or, as with my children, "What do you want to do in dreamland?" or "Whom do you want to take with you into dreamland?" Dreamland is popular with my children because dreams are very special to us; sharing our dreams is another way that my daughters and I build our relationship. However, you don't need to talk about dreamland to get your children into meditation. Simply find out what's a popular or important theme for them and use that as an introduction.

Another way into meditation is to tell a story, the way grandma used to. Children don't often get that special kind of grandmotherly care these days, the kind when you know grandma has *nothing else to do but to be here for you.* That's the kind of atmosphere in which a child can enter into the flow of meditation.

A third way is to let children tell you what happened to them today. Perhaps their school team won the soccer match, or the science test was more difficult than expected. Getting ready for meditation is a good setting for getting rid of all such unhappy feelings and fostering happy feelings.

Actually, any theme works as an introduction to meditation, as long as it's clear to you and to the children that this is going to be a special one-to-one time for you and them. "Because you really care about me," the child thinks, "I can go into meditation, and eventually to sleep, happy."

Creating this special atmosphere of your fullest presence and care can also be done in a classroom. I might begin by suggesting that the children rest their heads on their arms on their desks, asking them to relax and listen, and telling them that this is a special time for us to be with each other and with Jesus.

You may also practice this kind of meditation with your spouse. Begin by holding each other and hugging each other, reaffirm your love for each other and God's love for you, then ask each other, "How did it go for you today?" Encourage each other to let go of angers, fears, worries, and the like, so that you can enter sleep together in an atmosphere of love and peace.

CHAPTER **4**

Some Confusions and Hesitancies

Is Meditation Good for Children?

People wonder if their children can learn to meditate. I answer with a simple *yes.* In fact, children are the best learners, since they have no negative prejudices about the process and they find it a quite natural activity.

Furthermore, people wonder if meditation is good for their children. Again, I answer unhesitatingly *yes,* because in meditation a child can learn to experience God from the inside. While there are many ways by which God is mediated to your child from without—vocal prayers, liturgies, tradition, history, and the teachings of faith—meditation gives your child a way to know and experience God more directly and gives him or her a direct experience of who God might be. It is a way for a child to touch God and be touched by God. It also complements and enriches all those other, more external, ways of finding God.

Some parents and teachers who themselves are unfamiliar with meditation fear that meditation may be dangerous for their children. Far from being harmful to them, meditation is much more likely to foster their physical, mental and spiritual development.

Physically, meditation has a quieting effect that reduces muscular tension, facilitates going to sleep, and trains children to become relaxed, a skill that will benefit them for the rest of their lives. Meditation generates a sense of physical well-being. It encourages children to think of themselves as healthy, whole human beings. I haven't done any scientific research on this, but my experience is that children who meditate get fewer colds and fewer ordinary illnesses than other children.

Psychologically, meditation develops a capacity to be attentive, to use the imaginative faculty, to let go of destructive feelings—all of which skills can be used throughout life, too. The thrust of meditation is toward psychological wholeness and oneness; if you were to imagine yourself as a pile of puzzle pieces, meditation helps you put the puzzle together. In meditation your mind is set free from the bondage of shoulds, you learn to nurture your own well-being; you are able to say, "I like myself." One young meditator at school stopped me in the corridor one day proudly announcing, "I can handle it, Mrs. Scheihing." When I asked her what it was, she said, "Some of the kids were teasing me about my mother getting divorced. But I can handle it." And indeed she could.

My daughter came to me one day hurt and sad because a classmate had said, "I like somebody else better than you." She and I reaffirmed the unbreakable spiritual bond between us which allowed her to rechannel her sadness energy into an affirmation between us rather than remain stuck in the lack of affirmation she felt from her classmate. Our secret saying when we need to redirect feelings into healthy channels is, "Don't get mad, get glad." In remembering the bond between us she found a glad way to channel her emotional energies.

Spiritually, too, meditation and centering help you grow by leading you beyond the confines of formalized prayer. When young persons on a totally formalized prayer diet say, "I'm tired of saying my prayers," I don't hear their words as a sign that they want to stop seeking God. My belief is they want to find God at a deeper, more personalized level than is usually possible with recited prayer as they know it. I hear their words as a request for help to grow spiritually.

Young people naturally want to find God, and meditation helps them do their exploration without limitation. Contemplative prayer releases one's natural potential for experiencing God spontaneously in the present moment. Furthermore, centering and contemplative interaction with God help develop an inner sense of one's self as valuable, lovable, capable, and graced uniquely and directly by God.

Many children have come to me after meditation expressing in their own words the sentiments of the assertive child who once informed his critical mother, "God made me and God doesn't make junk." Children experience this truth personally because in meditation God communicates it to them.

FEAR OF MEDITATION

In my experience children do not fear meditation. Some adults who are unfamiliar with meditation may have concern mostly because of *how* they've been taught and *what* they've been taught about prayer. For example, I invite children to do meditation lying on a carpeted floor—or even a gym floor, if that's all that's available. To most parents who were taught that kneeling or standing are the only postures for prayer, lying down seems unacceptable, perhaps wrong and even dangerous. I often tell parents that St. Ignatius Loyola liked to meditate on his back!

Again, since most parents were never taught ways of meditation and contemplation, they may feel that the prayer ways they learned were best and want only those ways taught to their children.

They are perhaps convinced it will be harmful to faith if their children do not learn these traditional prayer ways. My response is that effective ways of praying need not be either traditional or new; they may be both. I encourage children to learn traditional ways as well as new ones.

I stress that meditation helps build a child's relation to God, but it also nurtures a child's relation to others. Often when I get a free space of time at home in the evening, I sit down on my favorite living room chair only to find my two daughters in pajamas bringing out their comforter and two pillows to be near me. "Can we all meditate together?" they ask. Knowing I will say yes, they put on a recording of meditative music, turn out the lights, and light a candle. This "snuggle time," as we call it, is a time for us to be with God, but it is also a time for loving each other and ourselves. *Quality* time, not *quantity* time, is what is important and special to parents and children.

Quality time is so crucial to mutual loving between parents and children. Children know if you have time for them and if they are a priority for you at this moment. Priority quality time says, "I want to be with God and I want to be with you." Snuggle time is our special moment to experience God and each other *at the same time.* I have never had a family meditation like that where the children didn't go to bed happy.

They fall asleep saying, "I love you, Mom." And I know they feel good, whole, connected to each other and to me. And all of us are connected to God. To make us very aware of our connections to each other and to God, we often visualize an imaginative, stretchable, unbreakable thread connecting our three hearts. We first started doing this one Valentine's Day. The stretchable thread was my gift to them—a way of staying connected heart-to-heart so that we could send thoughts or feelings to each other. We call this "kything." (It rhymes with "tithing.") Because we often reaffirm this unbreakable connection, it remains a continual sense of mutual loving support among us.

When a child enjoys physical wholeness, psychological well-being and spiritual value, that child can love God spontaneously and effortlessly. That child can also then explore relationships with others, for love of God overflows into love for special human persons and the love energy in those relationships naturally overflows toward others until a loving network is formed.

To Know, Love, and Serve God

"All this physical and psychological growth for my children is fine," some parents might say, "but how does meditation help them to know, love, and serve God?"

It is especially true for children that the first step in normal psychological development is knowing and loving themselves, then knowing and loving other humans, and finally God. Usually, however, all three steps are happening at the same time.

Meditation offers a unique way of *knowing God*. While the Bible and religion classes tell you *about* God, in meditation you spend time *with* God by letting stories about Jesus come alive in your mind and heart. Instead of reading about Jesus in the boat, meditation puts you right into the boat. As an eighth grader explained it to me, "Jesus is not here physically today but somehow he keeps on being here more and more when I go into meditation to be with him."

Meditation also evokes *love for God*. When I once asked a young boy how he knew that Jesus loved him, the boy responded, "By the way he looks at me when I sit by him in the boat. Jesus understood the pain I felt when I had my appendix operation." For children, love is exchanged very concretely, in a look, in a word of understanding.

Meditation facilitates the *service of God* by the intensity of the personal relationship it generates. Children who meditate no longer usually do kindness and service out of guilt, duty, or fear, but out of the intensity of their relationship to God. Meditation becomes a continuous call to love of neighbor. "God loves me so much," said a young boy, "that I've got a lot of love to spread around." Such a child begins to see his life and his relationships as a response to God's love for him. What a wonderful environment in which to consider one's future!

MEDITATION AND THE KINGDOM OF GOD

"But won't meditating make my children focus too much on themselves?" some parents wonder. "Won't it just make our children self-centered and narcissistic?"

"Not at all," I answer.

The objective of meditation, as of the gospel, is to help bring about the kingdom of God in human lives. This seems to me to require two focuses: Christ's word and its implications in my life. When I listen to what Christ in a gospel story is saying, for example, in the parable of the pearl, I also ask what the pearl is saying to me, or I may even "become" the pearl in meditation. Then I ask myself, "How is this pearl experience going to change my life?" Yes, there is growth in myself through meditation, but it is not self-centered; it is a response to Christ. When meditation is well-presented, it focuses not exclusively on me nor exclusively on Christ but on the relationship between Christ and me.

As history or a piece of the past, the Bible usually doesn't interest children, for they live primarily here and now. Through meditation, however, stories of Jesus can become living events. In their imaginations children can interact with Jesus today. They can find in him something relating to their own life—their pain, joy, discovery. While they may not understand the subtler theological nuances in biblical statements, they do understand that Jesus is for them, he gives them everything he has, and he loves them even when nobody else seems to.

When anyone enters into meditative relationship with Jesus, they soon discover that Jesus begins asking them to do something with the love, joy, and care he gives them. Personal response is called for by the gospel message and by meditation in Jesus' name: "My command is that you love others the way I love you," said Jesus. Children can and do respond to this invitation. Their caring response to others after meditation, for example, is a sign validating the reality of their meditative union with God.

MEDITATION FOR CHILDREN AND ADULTS

Meditation for children differs in a number of ways from meditation for adults. While children and adults may focus on the same thought, for example, the pearl of great price, the level of its meaning differs for children and adults because of their age and experience. In the pearl image, Jesus says to each meditator, "You are uniquely loved by me and I will give up everything to have you." What does *special* and *unique* mean to a child? What does it mean to an adult? What does giving up everything mean to an adult? To a child? Such questions naturally evoke different responses in adults and children.

Another difference between adults and children in meditation lies in the ability to relax, to let go, to flow, to become involved in the imagination and the senses. Relaxing, letting go, and imagining seem easier for children, probably because adults have more to let go of.

Four other reasons I've found that make meditation more difficult for adults include: (1) Adults seem to be preoccupied with what they *should* do or what is expected of them, more so than children. (2) Adults tend to look for results in meditation, while children are content simply to enjoy the experience, absorbing like a sponge whatever is there. (3) Adults sometimes feel the physical senses are a low-class gateway to learning, preferring intellect and higher reason, while children learn most of what they know through inner and outer sensory experience. (4) Finally, there are certain adults who want to do their thing on God (I don't know how else to say it), while children are content to let God do his thing on them.

A Few Cautions

Although I assert that meditation properly presented is not harmful to children, there are things to watch out for. First, if you are not going to guide your own children and meditate with them, be sure to inquire about the person who will be guiding them and facilitating their meditation process. In any profession there can be harmful practitioners. You can usually identify poor guides because, first of all, they tend to give negative input, which includes expressions that break down a child's well-being, harm a child's self-concept, or create suspicion, fear, or guilt in a child.

Second, beware of a guide who forces or imposes his or her meditative images on a child. In contrast, a good guide will offer positive suggestions and give options, choices, and alternatives by saying, "Here are some ways to begin your meditation. I offer them as suggestions. Follow whatever seems best for you." In this way the meditating child may choose what feels right.

Third, a guide can sometimes try to manipulate a meditative experience, controlling and directing it rather than letting the child get into the flow. My impression is that most guides who manipulate are simply afraid of the flow themselves. Once they realize the flow is leading the child into the very life of God and they can trust it, they are no longer held captive by the fear that leads to manipulation.

Actually, parents' mistaken attitudes toward meditation seem to be the most important things to watch out for, since these mistaken beliefs often tend to keep children from deeper meditative experience. Usually parental attitudes are not wrong, but merely limiting. For example, the parent who has very strict notions about what prayer should or shouldn't be can be very limiting. While formal prayers are clear and known, meditation in its deepest meaning involves secrets of the heart between the child and God. The unknown parts of their child can sometimes be a threat to parents. Again, some parents believe the mind and spirit have boundaries; in meditation, a child may go beyond all those presumed boundaries. Some parents like to have control over what their children say to God; in meditation, parents need to let go of such control and to invite their child, "Tell Jesus whatever you're feeling in your heart; you don't have to tell me what you say."

How to Help Your Children

In light of these mistaken and unhelpful attitudes, how can parents and teachers best help their children meditate? I have found general suggestions. The *first* is that parents and teachers themselves learn how to meditate so that they understand what meditation is and what happens when a person meditates. *Second,* to encourage children to meditate, adults will need to accept meditation as something important in their own lives. If meditation is important to you, it will tend to be valued by your children, but if meditation seems unimportant to you, your children will find it difficult to remain faithful to it. *Third,* I encourage parents and teachers to give priority to meditation in their own lives. If, for example, a parent's only meditation time is a few minutes after receiving communion, it really does not assume a priority. *Fourth,* if meditation is not important to you, then don't force your children to meditate, for it will probably tend to create a values conflict in them. Your children will find meditation for themselves somewhere someday. Even if you can't provide the way, the Lord will. Trust God in this matter.

The Fabric of Your Life

I am suggesting methods to help your children meditate and I invite you to join them in meditation. What I am telling you is that your full commitment to a life of prayer that includes meditation or contemplation will be the best impetus toward meditation you can give your child. What I am asking you to do—and what I am continually asking myself to do—is to integrate meditation into the fabric of your life. You are called to meditation, just as your children are. If you doubt your call, then try this simple experiment. Allow yourself to get deeply at peace, have nothing else to do for an hour and give yourself totally to listening to the Spirit's inner movements in your body and mind. I believe that you will feel an inner need at the roots of your being and you'll know you are called to a one-to-one relationship with God.

But you will probably cry out as I do, "Lord, I have no time!" I have heard myself making that disclaimer not only to God but to my children and my closest friends. Every now and then the irony of that excuse hits me: If I am saying that I have no time for the most important persons in my life, then where am I spending my time? Am I so much a slave to security, power, money, and unconsciousness that I would abandon the gift of friendship and the gift of love? I need quiet time, alone with my God, with my children, with my friends. And I want that kind of time often, every day. In today's world, such time is not structured into the normal day. Time is a luxury for me as a single working parent. I find I must make time and establish my priorities.

Once meditation becomes a priority in your life, many things will start to happen to you. You discover an energy source whose reserves fill your day. You discover a centering in your life that gives new meaning and enthusiasm to what you do. You discover your life threads weaving together into an integrative pattern. If meditation becomes genuinely valuable to you, your children will sense the transformation it generates in you and they will be attracted to it, too.

Part Two

MEDITATION:
HOW DO YOU TEACH IT
TO CHILDREN?

CHAPTER **5**

The First Steps

How Old Must a Child Be to Meditate?

This is not any easy question to answer. My rational mind says that as a rule children are ready for meditation as soon as they can understand a fairy tale and identify with one of its characters.

However, I know instinctively and intuitively that children can and do meditate much earlier than that. Why do I say this? The primary experience in meditation is one of utter trust in a person with whom you feel close and safe, for when you know a relationship is safe you can let go completely. And very young children can do this. In meditation you entrust yourself completely to God in a one-to-one relationship. But whether a relationship is with God, with a human person, with an animal or with a part of nature, as long as the letting go involves a complete trusting in the other, it shows that you are capable of deep meditative experience.

How Does a Child Develop This Sense of Safety and Trust?

I was talking to a thirteen-year-old who told me one of the most precious things in her life is time alone with her father. Her desire to be alone together with him is similar to the attraction of meditation. I would say that this young woman is ready to explore a one-to-one relationship with God if she wants to. A relaxed atmosphere of receptiveness is the place where a breakthrough in relationship can best happen, whether it is between a child and a parent or a child and God.

Different people have different ways of finding places of safety and trust. Once when my older daughter Maria was feeling out of sorts I asked her what we could do together to make her feel comfortable. She asked if we could sit alone together by our favorite old oak tree in the hills. I sat quietly by her there while she enjoyed being with the tree. She knew she could be totally trusting with nature there. Her relationship with that tree—being alone together with it—was a meditative experience; God brought safety and comfort to her through it.

From the beginning children typically are introduced to a meditative experience, unconsciously for the most part, when they are being held and rocked and sung to. At such time the child's experience is one of being alone together in an atmosphere of utter safety, trust, and love. That's the fundamental meditative experience, too. If your children have known being rocked and sung to, they will never entirely forget it, and when they begin to meditate they may recognize an old familiar feeling.

On the other hand, children who have not known trust and safety feelings, even with trees and other parts of nature, may find it difficult to let go into a meditative experience. If the outside world is scary and there is no place where a child can feel utterly safe, it is not likely that such a child will easily enter the inner world of meditation, especially if he or she does not know where this will lead.

CAN PARENTS AND TEACHERS MEDITATE WITH THEIR CHILDREN?

My assumption is that children learn to meditate best by doing it with loving adults. A bond of utter trust established between you and your children is the best model for a meditational relationship between your child and God. When you care enough to meditate with your children, you communicate that they are more important to you than anything else at this time. Experiencing your total presence allows them to hear God's wish to be totally present to them whenever they meditate.

Can Hyperactive Children Meditate?

Many parents and teachers assume that hyperactive children cannot do centering and meditation. Hyperactive children themselves are often convinced they can never keep their fingers and toes still enough to meditate as other children do. But they can.

In my experience, the ways of centering and meditating suggested in this book work as effectively with hyperactive children as with others, though it usually takes a bit longer for the hyperactive ones to grasp the idea of centering and inner relaxing. "Quietness comes from the *inside*," I tell them, "rather than from the outside or from someone else saying, 'Stop fidgeting!' " Once children realize there is an inner way of keeping fingers and toes still—a way that has nothing to do with "self-control" or will power—they are on their way to becoming good meditators. Usually it helps to give such children lots of support and to show loving confidence as they make their first meditation attempts.

As I was meditating one day with a group of children, there was a child whose hands and feet were continually moving. Not only was his body jerking, but he also couldn't stop giggling or laughing. Naturally, his restlessness began to disturb other children, dispelling the general atmosphere of silence and reverence. The boy himself was embarrassed at his lack of self-control.

Since he was a child I had worked with in counseling and

with whom I had built up trust, I simply went up to him and stayed at his side while I narrated the meditation. As my voice invited all the children to close their eyes, I moved my hand gently over his face as if symbolically brushing his eyes closed. As I asked all the children to quiet their hands and fingers (for *all* children are fidgety), I moved my hands over his hands and fingers gently touching them. And it worked. My touch enabled him to get in touch with his inner quietness.

Of course, the personal counseling relationship he and I had built up gave me the freedom to touch him and gave him the freedom to accept my touch. My voice did not show anger toward him; my gentle touch convinced him that my words were not a demand but an invitation.

Even from the little meditative work I've done with hyperactive children, I would suggest the following.

First, allow hyperactive children a longer time than usual to get into a relaxed state before meditation.

Second, if possible, build a relationship of rapport and trust with the child ahead of time. Thus, when during meditation you suggest "floating on a cloud," "feeling like a marshmallow," or "puffing up like a balloon," the anxious child has heard these suggestions beforehand and feels somewhat prepared for the experience. Such buildup eases a child into the process.

Third, working successfully with hyperactive children has something to do with humor during preparation time. Smile and laugh your way into the preparations for meditation. Don't be demanding or even extremely serious with your children. After all, you are inviting them into an enjoyable moment with God.

In general, while it is difficult to capture the attention of a hyperactive child, it is more difficult to keep it for any extended length of time. However, once a hyperactive child is able to experience being centered, that child will probably be better able to hear your directions and suggestions. The more relaxed and centered children get, the more receptive they seem to be. It's as if once a child is centered, he or she can begin to absorb necessary information or instructions. One reason children can open their minds is because they have become quiet inside.

How Can I Predispose My Child to Meditation?

Last December I asked my daughter Maria what she wanted for Christmas. She began with a few typical gift items like dolls and records, but then she stopped, looked at me, and said, "Do you know what I really want, Mom? I want to spend more time being alone with you and meditating with you." What I'm trying to say is doing meditation needn't generate a "have to" feeling but, as with Maria, it can have a "want to" feeling.

Meditation doesn't work with parents and children unless the parents are at peace with themselves. When you live on the fringe of burnout or hysteria, you can't make meditation happen. It has to flow. You have to want it to flow. Since the flow comes from inside, if the inside is in chaos then what's inside can't flow out freely.

Because of strain resulting from knee surgery, I found it difficult to find time for meditation during my recovery period. My children frequently asked me when I would be able to spend more time with them "having fun together." Just before Easter I told them I had a great surprise to share with them. "I've rented a cottage on the coast for a week," I told them, "and I'm going to take both of you to the ocean for a vacation. No television, no telephone. Nothing to interrupt us. Just us being together."

Then I asked them what they might like to do while we were there. They wanted to walk on the beach, to build sand castles, to read, to snuggle—and, "Can we lie down on the floor and listen to music and meditate together?" asked Angela.

I became choked up when I heard their request calling me back to quiet time together and meditation in my own life.

How Can I Introduce My Child to Meditation?

You might begin by reading some books or articles on meditation for children or by finding a workshop on meditation to learn about it first hand. You might talk to your children about your interest in exploring meditation and perhaps find a children's book that contains meditational reflections. Any religious bookseller can help you find the right books for your children.

Of course, the best way to introduce your children into meditation is to lead them there yourself. This means you accept your own call to meditation and then let your child be attracted by you. One parent told me, "At first I began reading about meditation, and with a little encouragement from a friend I began exploring this form of prayer I had never been taught. I hoped it would become meaningful to me and my family . . . it worked."

How Can I Motivate My Children to Meditate by Themselves?

I never came across a child who actively didn't want to meditate, that is, who didn't want to be alone together with God in a loving, trusting relationship. Some children, I admit, may have tried a meditation experience and felt bored, or said they didn't understand what they were supposed to do, or didn't like the particular experience they had, or found the process difficult because they had never done it before. But none of them said they didn't want to have a one-to-one relationship with God.

While children who are riddled with self-doubt or have a hopelessly poor self-concept might find meditation difficult because the letting go involves taking a risk, you can motivate most children simply by suggesting that meditation is something good for them and fun, a way of meeting Jesus personally and getting to know him closely. I often tell students that meditation is spontaneous and exciting, not boring and dull.

I can't stress enough the motivational impact of getting centered and doing meditation together with your children; besides, for them there is always the added benefit of getting special time alone with mom or dad.

How Do I Explain to Other Parents What Meditation Means to Me and My Children?

Since most parents or teachers you talk to will probably not be familiar with meditation, the first thing to explain is how meditation differs from other forms of praying with which they are familiar. You might begin by saying, "There are many different ways of experiencing God—singing hymns, reading the Bible, going to church, reciting prayers. Meditation, another way to God, differs from the rest in that it builds a two-way relationship with God. We've all been raised to *talk* to God, but most of us haven't been taught how to *listen* to God. *Meditation's way involves learning to hear God's voice from the inside.* In contrast, when you say the Lord's Prayer, for example, you may feel you have done something: you've talked to God and maybe asked for something. Saying the Lord's Prayer may feel like something you *should* do. In meditation, it's as if God replies to you and there are no shoulds; in meditation, you listen as well as speak to God."

Another thing you might want to emphasize in talking to other parents is how meditation puts you and your children in contact with God. You might say, "In meditation I ask my child to picture Jesus in imagination, to touch him, hug him and sit next to him in a boat. When you love people you want to be with them, and meditation is where this happens. It provides a way for a child to have Jesus present right there in imagination and even have a conversation with him. I tell my children that sometimes in meditation it may seem as though nothing is happening, but the more you let go and trust, the more you realize you feel closer to God and are getting to know God personally."

You may also wish to share with other interested adults how meditation introduces your children to silence, a quiet place, a special quality time together, and an awareness that you want to be with them. Through holding, touching, and music you prepare your children for a God encounter by creating an atmosphere of closeness, relaxation, and readiness to sense God's presence.

CHAPTER 6

Some Practical Points

WHERE AND WHEN TO MEDITATE?

Meditation happens best in an atmosphere of quiet and trust. For my children, at home before bedtime with the least amount of distractions proves again and again to be the best meditation setting. One thing you cannot do is meditate alongside distractions and noise; for example, you can't meditate in the family room when the television set is on or the dog keeps marching through. In summertime, we have enjoyed meditating outside in the garden and yard. Once we meditated in sleeping bags under the stars.

With a group of children at school, an atmosphere of silence and trust may be created by a teacher in a classroom or in a special setting. At our school, we began the LISTEN program when we realized children's need to experience quiet time with God. We studied a child's typical day and discovered that from 7 A.M. to 7 P.M. a child usually has no quiet time at all. "At least when you go the bathroom you're alone," I suggested to a fourth grader. "Not in my house," was his reply. "My brother always comes in."

Decades ago, children in parochial schools were sent to the church "to make a visit," as we called it then. That was a quiet time for us. LISTEN tried a new way of achieving that same quiet feeling. Each day in each grade the teacher created a quiet atmosphere for five minutes, ceasing all academic work. What happened in each classroom then was not a religion class, for there was no formal doctrinal instruction. It was a five-minute period simply for silently sharing your feelings with Jesus.

Those few meditative minutes turned out to be very special in helping children understand many religious teachings. For example, during formal religion classes, church doctrine about the Eucharist and the transformation of bread and wine into the body and blood of Christ could be taught to children conceptually. During LISTEN time, however, children could be contemplatively present at the Last Supper table with Jesus and the apostles. In those moments, imaginatively and emotionally, they could re-experience the words and actions of Jesus celebrating the first holy communion service. Children seemed to grasp the meaning of the Eucharist and other doctrines more fully when they could experience the original doctrinal moment with Jesus in meditation.

Sometimes teachers suggested themes for talking to Jesus; sometimes teachers invited children to get in touch with whatever was on their minds and share it while quietly keeping company with God.

"Love is special to every now," was LISTEN's motto, the now referring to those daily five minutes of silence with Jesus. The notion of silence in an academic setting was brand new to children. The notion of silence as a prayer form was also brand new to children. When teachers were enthusiastic and excited about the LISTEN program, students responded well. When teachers didn't value the silence or the meditation, children tended to follow suit.

Providing a satisfying time for meditation at home or school is difficult. For parents or teachers in charge, meditation either is or isn't a priority. Meditation happens best when it is not a time emotionally sandwiched in, but a time set apart, made special.

How Long and How Often Should Children Meditate?

The length of an experience depends on the situation. For example, in a classroom with young children just learning meditation, three minutes daily is probably enough. As time goes on and as the children's skills develop, the meditation period may be gradually increased. Ten minutes daily, however, would be a maximum for classroom settings, except when meditation is done in conjunction with a longer ceremony.

When working with your own younger children at home, meditate for ten minutes more or less as often as possible. Daily is best. No one, as far as I know, has developed a general procedure for training children to meditate in the Christian tradition. So I answer the length of meditation question simply from my own experience.

What's an Attractive Way to Get Started?

When first introducing meditation to children, begin by telling them a story. Choose a once-upon-a-time fantasy that allows for much imaginative response. Ask children to visualize the story, reminding them they have a second set of senses—seeing, hearing, smelling, tasting, touching—inside their imagination. Suggest that the children, as St. Ignatius Loyola tells meditators, "picture in your imagination the people in the story, hear their words, watch their actions." Let children watch the story unfold within themselves. Invite them to become a part of the story, to dialogue with the characters, to feel what they are feeling, to respond with feelings of their own. As I mentioned before, meditation offers a way of learning religious truths by experiencing them with feelings in imagination.

For children, guidance at the start of a meditation is usually helpful, but once the drama begins spontaneously unfolding in the child's feelings and imagination, the adult guide need not offer any further directions except to encourage the child's spontaneous meditative process, listening to God and keeping company with God.

WHAT DOES LISTENING IN PRAYER, OR KEEPING COMPANY WITH GOD, MEAN?

Listening to God means learning how to hear God from the inside. It means recognizing how God communicates directly to us through inner senses and through feelings God inspires in us. On a level beyond feelings, there is a kind of listening I call perceiving; it happens when you are able to sense a divine presence, the voice of God as a presence inside you.

In meditation you talk to God but also allow God time to talk to you. So after you talk, allow yourself to be open, receptive, trusting. God usually doesn't reply in normal human ways, but in images, feelings, sensations. Sometimes in meditation you have no idea what is happening; you can't imagine that anything important is happening, but you continue to believe that something is happening. To foster such belief, you might picture yourself as a dry lake waiting to be filled, or your mind as a blank screen upon which God will place some image. To listen to God, then, involves letting yourself enter that image. Sometimes such listening invites you to bring something to action, to do something.

Listening like this or keeping company with God is a skill that takes weeks, months, or even years to learn, but with consistent practice you learn to have a clearer sense of God's presence and the Spirit's inner movements in you.

You can help children develop their inner listening skills by asking them in silence to listen to their own feelings and sensations, for example, "How are you feeling right now?" "Where in your body do you locate that feeling?" "What other feelings did you have today?" "How does it feel inside your nose when you inhale?" "What do you feel happening inside your chest when you breathe?" And so on.

Once children become comfortable within, you may invite them to begin listening for God's response in their feelings and imaginations. You may ask them, for example, "What does Jesus' face look like?" "What is God asking you to do to love him today?" "What feelings does Jesus have in this story?"

Don't expect children to "hear" God the first time that they meditate. In the beginning you should be pleased if you can simply get them to grow quiet, let go of most distractions, and let their minds become like an empty screen. Perhaps next you can help them become aware of their breathing, their feelings, their inner activity. Take time with them and be patient. Learning to listen to the interior world is like learning to play a musical instrument. Music is a language wholly different from the words and sentences of ordinary speech. So too is the language of the interior world.

HOW IMPORTANT IS POSTURE IN MEDITATION?

For children, because their meditation periods are usually short, the posture they take doesn't really matter as long as they're comfortable. Remember that comfort is different for each person, so allow children to make individual decisions about their preferred postures. Health and energy seem to flow most freely through the body when the spine is erect, which can happen, for example, sitting, standing, lying on one's back. The spine can remain erect when kneeling also, but most children find kneeling an uncomfortable posture. Invite your children to explore different postures, especially with erect spine, but don't force them to use a posture that feels uncomfortable to them.

How Does Relaxation Help a Child to Meditate?

Physical relaxation and mental calmness are prerequisites to successful meditation. Children cannot hear the voice of God when their bodies are tense and fidgety and their minds are spinning distractedly. When children sleep, their bodies and minds relax. Sleep and relaxation are natural states. This is especially noticeable with hyperactive children who can't sit still but must be in and out of their chairs, constantly moving around—until they start to fall asleep. Then they relax.

You can help some children relax by having them suggest to each part of their body to take a siesta for the next five minutes. Suggest that they relax their fingers, letting their fingers get quiet and sleepy, then their arms, their toes, their legs, and so on. In this way, part by part they begin learning how to invite themselves to relax. Children feel good inside when they can begin to exercise that kind of conscious control over their bodies. Because meditation is meant to be enjoyable, it happens best when children are relaxed.

The imagination can also help facilitate relaxation by absorbing the mind. I often ask children to picture themselves floating on a cloud or on a river and encourage them to let their bodies feel the floating, too. This tends to relax them. I explain that for the next five minutes they don't *have* to do anything, they can just let go and be. Letting go control from the inside seems to make them feel lighter and more relaxed.

How Can I Help Children Prepare Their Bodies and Minds for Meditation?

The first steps in getting ready for meditation are always *relaxation* and *centering.* Both of these procedures can take a variety of forms.

I usually begin *relaxation* by asking children to become as comfortable as possible, wherever they are. Next, I ask them to close their eyes so they will be free of distractions. If clos-ing eyes feels threatening to certain children, I allow them to keep their eyes open; my objective is always primarily to help them be more comfortable.

Normally, I then suggest that they watch themselves breathing for a while. I might also ask them with every inha-lation to take in whatever is good and with every exhalation to let go of whatever they don't need to hold onto, things like worries, fears, anger, sadness. To focus on their breathing usually helps relax them.

Next comes *centering*. As their bodies grow still (sometimes this process takes most of the available meditation time, which is okay), you may help them clear their minds and tell them that as they do they will begin to sense God's presence within. I usually say something like, "You will recognize Jesus' presence, for it will have the same comforting feeling as when your mother rocked you and sang to you. You could tell by her touch and the very tone of her voice that she was communicating her love to you. Jesus will affect you in a sim-ilar way."

I might also remind children that Jesus' messages often don't sound like a human voice—"as when I talk to you"—but Jesus will communicate in his own ways, and if you just stay quiet and open you'll know it when he speaks.

At this point I usually present the *meditation theme*, if I haven't presented it before. Presenting the theme is the third step in meditation. Often the theme involves reading from the Bible or telling a biblical story.

Before the meditating with music begins, I suggest that the children ask God for a gift. This is the step I call *petition*. By asking for a specific grace—to be kind to others today, to know Jesus better, to play happily and without fighting—the direction and purpose of a meditation becomes clear and fo-cused.

An Example of Getting Children Ready for Meditation

Last Advent, the children at St. Eugene's Elementary School were getting ready to attend an evening candlelight service in the church next door. I wanted them to experience the service meditatively, so I prepared them in the classroom ten minutes ahead of time as if they were about to begin a meditation. Here are the words I used. You'll notice the preparation stages—relaxation, centering, theme, and petition—are included in order.

The Light of Christ

Relaxation. "I would like you to put your head on your desk and close your eyes.

"For the next few minutes I want you to relax your mind and body and begin to prepare yourself for the candlelight service tonight.

"Take a deep breath. . . breathe out. Another breath. . . very quietly. And begin to sense a calmness coming over your whole being. You don't have to listen to my voice. You can go wherever your mind takes you. You don't have to listen to me with your conscious mind because your inner mind will be listening to everything I say."

Centering. "Now I would like you to see a candle in your imagination. Perhaps it is a candle you will see tonight at church. It can be any size, color, or shape you like. Now watch the flame begin to burn. See the flicker of light as it dances against the shadows. Maybe you see other images in the candlelight. If you do, allow your senses to absorb all the images the light offers to you. Very soon now you will begin to feel the warmth of the candle enter your body. Feel it as it fills your head and comes down your face. Notice how relaxed all the muscles around your eyes, nose, mouth, and neck have become. Let this warmth travel down through your body, fill your chest and lungs, your back, your stomach, all your internal organs. Feel the warmth between your legs and in your knees, in your ankles and each toe."

Theme. "Now that you have experienced the gentle warmth and flow of your candlelight in your own being, watch what happens as you begin to shed your own ray of light to the person next to you. Your warmth reaches out and touches another person and brings light and loveliness to one, two, three, four persons, and on and on and on. See yourself aglow with the light of Christ, radiating the brilliance of his love, warming the hearts of all those near to you."

Petition. "And if you allow yourself, you will experience a very special kind of magic this evening at church, especially with the music and singing. At some point tonight—I don't know when, but you will know when—you can ask God for the gift to realize that Christ is the light of the world and that he has touched you and set your spirit aglow with the radiance of his love. And you will be an 'Alleluia' from head to toe.

"You may now open your eyes and keep these thoughts quietly in your mind as we walk silently over to church."

How Can Music Help My Child Meditate?

I use music playing in the background to facilitate meditation whenever I can, at home or at school. Like a chemical catalyst, music seems to make meditation happen easier, faster, deeper. I can't imagine how I could help children to meditate as well without it.

Unquestionably, appropriate music heightens the meditative experience whether it's played on a million dollar stereo system or a child's cassette player. It invites children into a meditative state, evokes and heightens their imagination, and allows emotions to announce their presence powerfully. With music everything flows more easily; the drama of the meditative encounter is intensified. Never judgmental, music invites you and calls you to follow. During meditation, music powerfully works its innate soothing and healing effects in children.

How Do I Choose Music to Play While My Children Meditate?

The most important criterion for selecting meditative music is *mood* or *feeling tone.* Does the music's mood consistently support the mood of the meditation? If it does, then it will probably be helpful. For example, if you want to spend a peaceful time with Jesus, choose quiet and soothing music. On the other hand, if you want to meditate on Jesus' anger when he chased the money changers from the temple, gentle music will not be helpful. Instead use music whose mood is violent, strong, and assertive.

You can find music to fit any mood. Music teachers and sales people at record stores can help you select appropriate music. My meditation-with-music cassettes for children may give you an idea of how to select music for meditation.

You may use the same musical selection again and again at different times for different scenes, as long as the music's mood corresponds with that of the meditation. A variety of musical selections which may be helpful in facilitating meditation and centering with children are suggested on pp. 101–2.

I find classical music consistently effective for facilitating meditation, even with children who have not been brought up listening to it. I must also say I have used most other kinds of music as well—folk, popular, choral, rock, jazz, even electronic music.

Desite the almost miraculous holistic power of music to catalyze meditation and contemplation, the most necessary element of successful meditation, I repeat, is the child's feeling safe, trusting, and open to the flow. Music will call a child powerfully and deeply into relationship with God, in the same way that mother's lullaby calls a child to go with the flow, only if the child has reached an inner place of trust and openness.

A Child's Center

There's one thing to really respect when you deal with children: their center. Each child is sacred ground and somewhere in that sacred ground is a sacred temple, a sanctuary. That sanctuary is a child's center, or soul. It is a place where the child and God meet. No other person knows where a child's sacred center is, no one but the child and God. It's a private space in you that can be entered by you and by God. No one else, no matter how hard they try, can force themselves into your center. When somebody loves you, they help you preserve your center and enrich it. When somebody hates you, they may try to invade your center, attempt to destroy it, tell you it's not important, or get you to abandon it.

The problem is that many children are not conscious that they possess a center. Others don't know how to make contact with it. So, somewhere in the beginnings of meditation, I try to help children find their center; this process is called centering.

Sometimes I do centering using a road symbol. "There is a road inside you," I begin. "You may not know where it leads, but if you follow it, it will take you to a place where you and God are going to meet together." I use metaphors and symbols to help children maintain their centering process. I tell them, "Of course, I know there is no road inside you and that your center is not really in some physical place like your lungs, liver or spleen. But I use these images to help you discover the experience of your center. Once you've identified this 'place' and your body, mind, and spirit are aware of it, then you are centered. Often we lose contact with our center, so we need to do centering again and again in order to get re-centered."

The important thing for any parent or teacher to remember is that there is no trespassing on this sacred ground with any child, even one of your own flesh and blood. You may guide children to their center and tell them to watch for God there, but you can't go in, unless invited. Everyone must wait to be invited into that space to which God and your child give birth.

What Does it Mean to Enter Another's Center or to Have Another Person Enter Your Center?

Your center is important because there in that sacred place is where all the real action happens with God. The action is you and God giving birth to something special—a relationship that can overflow with love for the entire world. Once this relationship is created, you can invite other people (other centers) into it; when you connect with someone center-to-center, it is called kything.

Once a child knows how to get centered—to go to that sacred place created by God and the child—you may teach the child how to kythe, that is, how to invite another's center into their sacred place, or to become centered in another's center. I taught my children to kythe with me and with each other by using our Valentine unbreakable love thread as a symbol of our center-to-center connection.

In order for me to kythe with you, that is, to join our centers, you must have a place you and God gave birth to, and I must have a similar place God and I gave birth to. When either of us loses that sacred place (when we become uncentered) we can't actively kythe with each other, because there wouldn't be a place from which to kythe. When I drop my children off at school in the morning we often say, "Bye. I love you. Kythe with me today."

How Does Meditation Help My Children Relate to the Larger World?

Meditation, when it involves a deep encounter with God, happens at your center. In a sense, God is always in that sacred place waiting. You simply choose to go there or not. When you do go there to meet God, you will be affected by the experience. You will never be the same person coming back to the outer world that you were going in.

It is the adult guide's challenge to help children who have met God at their center to understand what they have experienced and to share with others the energy, love, and gifts they received from God there. In our Christian tradition, we believe that God's gifts to individual members of the community are always meant for the benefit of the community as well as of the individual. In other words, God's gifts to us are meant to be shared. This process of coming back to the outer world and sharing the gifts of God received in meditation transforms meditation from a possible narcissistic practice to one that helps build a loving community that brings about the kingdom.

What are Some Typical Responses of Children to Meditation?

When children describe a successful meditation experience, they might say things like, "I like that!" "When can we go there again?" "I felt safe there." "I didn't know my mind could go that far!" "How did it happen, Mommy?" "I saw all sorts of things."

I usually confirm their experiences by saying, "Now that you know what it feels like in meditation—safe, exciting, loving, new—you can feel those feelings again and again. That's the gift of Jesus' presence."

Once they've experienced Jesus and his gifts in meditation, it is part of their memory bank, and like any experience, they can recall it whenever they want to. For children, meditation provides a reservoir of happy memories with Jesus, like memories of being with a best friend. Just as it's fun to remember things that happened with friends and to share them with others, it's fun to remember things that happened with Jesus and to share those experiences with others.

How Do I Evoke Sharing Responses from Children After Meditation?

Never force a child to share what happened in meditation. Their experience may be so deep and private that it is meant for no one else but them. Even when an experience isn't profound or private, some children prefer not to share what happened or did not happen. Respect their privacy, especially if they are in a group of children.

For children who are willing or at least less reluctant to share, you can facilitate their responses by asking open-ended leading questions, for example, "How did it feel during the music?" "What did you do with Jesus?" "Where did you go?" "What did you see?" "What feelings did you have?" "How did your body respond?"

It is important to remember that different children go to different depths in meditation. Be accepting of whatever responses they give. Don't challenge or deny their responses. Don't undervalue what they say, since ultimately you really never know what they have experienced. Even if they are willing to share their meditation with you, they may be limited by their vocabulary and experience from describing what happened in any adequate way.

As a guide, however, you may reinforce their positive comments as an incentive to keep exploring meditation. You may also focus on their insights, awarenesses, good feelings, or other gifts that they received in meditation and gently spell out the value and usefulness of these gifts to their family, friends, and others. You can begin giving them a sense that their gifts are meant to be shared with and overflow into the community. For them, of course, their primary communities are their families and their classmates. Meditation will usually offer them new ways of accepting, understanding, and loving these people in their lives.

CHAPTER 7

Further Questions

How Can You Guide Children to Their Inner Selves?

Trust is the first thing that must be established in the relationship between guide and meditator. Remember, you cannot force children to go inside themselves; you may only invite them to go inward.

Children who are not yet at a place of trust—they may not trust themselves—need to be left free to do something else. If a class or group is meditating, find something for an untrusting child to do that won't disturb others.

Once children trust you and themselves, they can let go to the flow of meditation without fear of getting hurt or lost. In cases where trust is fragile, it may be helpful physically to take the child's hand in order to help the child feel secure enough to begin an imaginative journey inside. Here I might begin by saying, "You don't have to be afraid. I won't let anything happen that might hurt you. I'll hold your hand. You may even take me with you on your journey if you wish, or call me to be with you at any time. What you'll discover will be very lovely. You are free to discover anything you want to that is good for you. You may bring back a whole treasure of things."

When you guide an individual child on a meditative journey, it's sometimes mind boggling to see what the child experiences whenever he or she is given permission to experience *anything*. You are watching the inner self at work.

Once you get to know your children in meditation, you begin to understand them at a deeper level and relate to them in new ways, for you are discovering insights about them that you never knew, wisdom that you didn't put there. How exciting to discover the otherness of your child!

How Can I Help Children Deal With Fears They Find When They Go Inside Themselves?

Meditation provides a way for children not only to uncover the wisdom that lies hidden inside, but also to get rid of unwanted feelings, attitudes, fears, and pains that clutter up inside. Begin a cleansing process by introducing Jesus and having the children ask him to take away their fears and pains. Remind them that children can throw away or give away an unwanted toy.

Toys are easily recognized. It's more difficult for children to tell you what's hurting inside, but in meditation suggest that they can give an unwanted feeling a name, a color, a sound, an identity. (They will use descriptions appropriate to their age.) Once they can identify it, they can begin dealing with it directly. No longer are they helplessly (and probably unconsciously) in its power.

Once they identify their unwanted feeling, you as guide can present them with a choice. "Do you still want to hold onto this feeling or do you want to let it go?" Let them decide. If they choose to let it go, then you can help them find a place and an imaginative way for disposing of it, for example, putting it in a garbage can, tying it to a rock and dropping it in the ocean, or grinding it up in a kitchen disposal.

Getting rid of harmful feelings is something you will always want to do in the company of Jesus. For example, invite the child to be in a boat with Jesus and together they can throw the identified feeling overboard. Or Jesus and the child may be standing on a mountaintop and together they throw the unwanted feelings over the cliff.

How Can Meditation Help Jesus Become My Child's Good Friend?

If you encourage children to do their inner cleansing with Jesus, then Jesus becomes real for them, a living person that they can talk to and listen to and, above all, *be with*. Children can bring Jesus into their bedroom today or go back to his era in history to be with him, for example, as he lives out a gospel story. In this way, a reciprocal relationship is built up in which Jesus and the children visit each other in their own times and places. In the end, children can honestly say, "Jesus is real and Jesus is my friend."

Meditation provides opportunities for children to meet Jesus and spend time with him in order to share with him the things happening in their lives. Something really special happens to children when they discover that Jesus is their best friend, that he is the person with whom they can share the center of their being.

One of the best benefits of meditation is the development of self-esteem and self-worth from within. My self-concept is enhanced and I know my worth as a person because I know I am loved by God. As one child put it, "Before I ever did meditation my teacher told me that Jesus loved me, but now I know it because I can feel it, just like I know my mother loves me by the way she touches me and hugs me."

How Can I Help Children Develop Their Inner Senses?

Meditation happens more easily and more enjoyably when children are in touch with the activity happening inside them—in their body, feelings, mind, imagination, and at their center. Developing inner senses is a skill that takes practice and can be fun.

I do it with my children as if it were a game. I presume most parents do these kinds of games naturally, so I'm sure I'm not telling you anything new. I begin with the obvious senses the child knows about. I suggest, for example, "With the eyes of your imagination let's explore. Perhaps you'd like to go to a favorite part of your body and look around. Then tell me what you see."

After they tell me what they "see," I bring in the other familiar senses. "Bring your inner ears down into your stomach and listen to the sounds they make. Tell me what you hear." Or "Take your imagination's fingers and smooth out some rough, tired muscles in your arms and legs. Then tell me what you did." Create similar enjoyable tasks for the inner sense of smell and taste, too.

This way into a child's interior world invariably proves successful. Once your children become familiar with this inner space, begin to talk about the thousands of senses that have not yet been named and studied scientifically. If children look puzzled when I suggest that there are many unnamed senses, I reply, "You know what they are! It's not important to give them names, but you can if you want to because then we can talk about them."

If they still look puzzled, I might say, "I'll tell you a few of these new senses I've identified. See if you recognize them. First, there's the inner sense that tells you somebody likes you even though they've never come right out and said it. Second, there's the inner sense that tells you when somebody doesn't like you. Do you recognize those two senses?" Next you can ask them to describe other unnamed inner senses. Be patient as they struggle to do the naming. It is an important moment for them.

Once they identify some of their inner senses, take every possible opportunity to let them trust those inner senses as surely as they trust their outer eyes and ears. Even though these new senses don't have names, they are real and come from an inner wisdom, for they are gifts of God. Learning to trust those senses—or intuitions, as we sometimes call them—and to act on them is a way of making the wisdom gained in meditation useful in the outer world.

Another inner skill useful in meditation that can be developed by practice is fantasy, or creative imagination. Talk about fantasy with children and invite them to take frequent fantasy trips and to do it consciously.

Yet on another side of the inner life are feelings. Help children to recognize and identify feelings. Once they learn to notice obvious feelings such as joy, love, peace, fear, anger, hatred, shame, embarrassment, jealousy, and the like, they will begin to refine their feeling sense. They might notice subtle changes in feelings. Perhaps they will even recognize two or more feelings—even opposite ones like anger and love—existing at the same time. God often speaks to us through feelings, so it is helpful to be familiar with feeling language.

Finally, you can combine different activities of the inner world. For example, you can invite your heart to have a conversation with your big toe, or you can have each of your inner senses act out some drama in your imagination.

In developing inner senses, it is very valuable to invite children to share their experiences and discoveries. The struggle to *name* inner experience will pay off well in years to come, not only in deeper meditation but in a more conscious living of everyday life.

CAN CHILDREN MEDITATE ON THE BIBLE?

While children can read the Bible and listen to sermons about its meaning, meditation and contemplation offer practical ways of getting inside the Scriptures and learning about God in direct experiential interaction. While religious teachers may tell you what the Bible means to them, meditation allows you a way to discover what it means to you. It allows the Bible to speak to you in a very personal way.

Again and again I find through meditation that children are able to grasp deep religious teaching and doctrine very clearly and concretely. Children understand theological truths about Jesus directly when they encounter him at the core of their being while meditating on a biblical event.

One of the best ways children meet Jesus in the Bible is through parables because Jesus used parables to explain who he was and what he was doing. During meditation you can enter a parable in your imagination and let it come alive inside you. You can become a part of the parable and let it become a part of you. For example, when Jesus says the kingdom of heaven is like yeast which a woman kneaded into two cups of flour, let yourself become the yeast or let the yeast come inside you as if you were the cups of flour mixed with the yeast. Identify with the parable event in some way in order to find out what Jesus is saying about himself in the story. If a meaning is not clear, even when you experience yourself as yeast or flour, then picture Jesus inside you and ask him yourself what the parable tells about him.

At the end of a Sunday liturgy I sometimes ask a number of children what the gospel reading was about. Usually they can't remember. However, when I invite children beforehand, for example on Friday, to enter the Sunday gospel story in meditation, giving them a chance to identify with it, then on Sunday when they hear it read from the pulpit, they remember it vividly.

I also encourage priests and ministers familiar with meditation skills to invite congregations into a meditative homily, encouraging them to relax and let the story come alive in their imaginations.

In some cases children will find it helpful, when a gospel image is not familiar to them, if you suggest a contemporary related image. For example, fig trees are not a familiar experience to today's children, so you may substitute the name of another fruit-bearing tree. Likewise, old-fashioned fish nets are not a common item in today's world, so find an image of something contemporary in which we gather or haul things. If you can't think of a suitable substitute, ask the children themselves.

How Can I Help Children Create Their Own Personal Meditations?

The simplest way to help children become independent meditators, so that they can meditate even when you are not around to guide them, is to teach them a basic formula for meditation.

The one I use tells children there are three basic stages in a meditation: *getting ready, meditating,* and *reviewing.* These stages are developed and described more fully in the following chapter.

Because getting ready includes a number of steps, it may seem complicated at first, but after you and your children have practiced meditating a number of times, the steps will flow together naturally. Besides, you don't have to do all the steps every time. Remember children are natural contemplatives. For your convenience, I present each meditation in Part III using this basic formula.

You might want to emphasize with children how meditation seems to work best when they focus on one image, one story, one thought, one symbol, one phrase, or even one word. Once they choose their single focus, they can ask themselves, "What do I see, hear, and feel?" "Where am I?" "Who is with me?" If they have some favorite pieces of music for meditation, encourage them to use one of them.

What Role do Symbols Play in Meditation?

Children know how symbols work because in their games and play they are always symbolizing: Mother's antique bedspread becomes a royal cloak, an old toy wagon becomes a shiny new car, a rag doll becomes a living child upon whom is bestowed love and affection. Symbols like these can open children up to explore nonordinary levels of consciousness. In a similar way symbols associated with Jesus, such as the manger, the cross, or symbols from his parables, can lead children into deeper spiritual levels of understanding. Often a single image such as a rainbow or a butterfly can unlock much spiritual awareness in children. Looking at a symbol or holding it in our hands—a candle, a palm branch, a painting, an old family Bible—calls us beyond the thing we see or touch, rekindling important memories or creating a longing for the future. With symbols we look at a physical thing and perceive unseen reality, perhaps many other realities.

Any object can become a symbol for children—a slice of bread, a seagull, an apple, a glass of water, a piece of clothing—as long as the object is open to other levels of meaning. Children respond easily and naturally to symbols, with understanding and feeling, provided they are invited to enter the world of the symbol, interact with the symbol, or even themselves become the symbol, as the child in imagination becomes the yeast in Jesus' parable.

There is usually no need to explain a symbol—a lighted candle, a darkened room, a mask—for each symbol communicates by itself. Preferably, a symbol is to be experienced rather than discussed if the symbol is to communicate life to a child.

Also, since symbols usually appear on their own without planning or programming, there is no need to force meaning into them or to force them into some desired meaning. When you sense the wisdom and energy of a symbol, you will know interiorly and intuitively the truth of your awareness.

Symbols, either tangible ones or ones that live only in the imagination, are commonly used as a focus for meditation. There are no limits to what objects can be symbols, no limits to what we can utilize in helping us find our way to God.

CHAPTER 8

Group Meditation

Is Group Meditation for Children Possible?

Yes. In fact, for some children it provides an easy and attractive introduction to meditation because of the supportive atmosphere created by the group.

When leading a group meditation longer than a few minutes, I find it preferable to do it outside a classroom whenever possible and convenient. I feel there is a need for children to let go of the academic environment in order for the group meditation to work well. Use any place that can provide an atmosphere of silence, for example, a church, an auditorium, or even outdoors.

How Can Group Meditation Be Helpful to Children?

It is definitely helpful to bring a group of children together. *First* of all, it makes children who meditate conscious of themselves, both as individuals and as group members. I invite children to share their feelings and experiences with each other to help them gain a sense of their own gifts and energies, as well as the gifts and energies of other group members. For example, near the end of a group meditation, I might ask children to be in touch with a nice feeling happening to them at the time and I ask them to choose a color to symbolize that feeling. "Fill yourself with that color," I suggest, "and when you're filled with it, send that color with its feeling to a person nearby you. Then add that person's color to yours. Pretty soon, if you all keep sending out your colors and adding them to your own, you'll all have a rainbow full of colors inside of you." Afterwards, I ask the children to name the color and feeling they began with. After many of them have shared, I point out how the rainbow they all possess represents the group's good feelings and energies, for the rainbow symbolizes a combination of all the personal experiences of God that happened in the room.

Second, sharing experiences verbally is itself helpful for children, for they discover there is no right or wrong answer. We simply want to know what that child experienced. Such nonjudgmental sharing helps children who would normally remain quiet because of a fear they might not know the "right answer." As one child explained, "You hear others feeling the same things you do, the same feelings you had inside."

Third, group meditation is a powerful teaching method—especially as a way of "experiencing" religious doctrine—because as a teacher you can utilize the reinforcement given by the group. Since all of the children shared this experience of group unity, you can refer again and again to that experience. For example, to a group that shared meditation and its energies together, I find it easy to talk about the communal nature of the Eucharist. "Remember the sense of unity and sharing we experienced in meditation together in the school hall?" I might begin. "There," I remind them, "we were able to give something like energy to each other. Even though we couldn't see it, we could feel it and picture it in our imaginations. So in communion we also feel a sense of unity, and we all can share our love for Jesus with each other. Even though we can't see Jesus inside us, we can feel his power and share it with others."

Fourth, you can invite children to experience themselves in a quiet, nonmoving, silent way, similar to the way they feel when they go to sleep at night. Learning to induce a sense of inner silence becomes an incentive, for it produces a good feeling. It reminds children, whose ordinary day is quite hectic, that they can relax themselves even when they are part of a group. It enables children to experience their own sounds of silence.

Fifth, group meditation (often the only chance for meditation some children ever get) allows a child to explore inner feelings in a group context. It's an exciting and new experience, for afterwards the group talks about experiences children usually never talk about. In the group, they are fostering their own imaginative development in an open-ended experience. Whenever you give children permission to explore a place where they haven't been before or one to which they'd like to go, it's a nice experience.

Sixth, when children come out of a meditative experience, they often feel good and valuable. "I experienced something good," was the simple way a third grader explained it to me. The unspoken, important part of that feeling was that it happened not in secret or when alone but in the context of the entire group.

Seventh, meditation in group helps children get in touch with their bodies and bodily responses. For example, you feel the beauty of your breath going in and out; you learn to focus on body experiences, even those that happen inside like heart beats, pulses and the rise and fall of the stomach in breathing. When a parent is leading an individual child in meditation, the parent can stroke the child's body and ask the child to relax and become aware of the bodily feelings. In a group, even without a parent's physical touch, a child can get in touch with the body's responses and self-healing capacities. I often have children tell me what they discovered about their body during meditation.

Eighth, after group meditation in the hall the children go into the school yard in a state of natural high. They seem less likely to fight, and an air of celebration seems to flow through the group. Meditation usually creates many positive feelings which tend to flow over into those with whom you interact.

How Do I Start a Group Meditation?

In getting the group ready, (1) invite the children to relax, (2) help them become aware of God's presence, and (3) encourage them to be open and trusting, especially in the presence of the group.

To help children relax, I most often use a physical relaxation procedure combined with some imaginative ways to relax. (Many specific ways of helping children relax may be found in the meditations in Part III.) I help them become aware of God's presence by connecting their belief in God with some physical process, such as heartbeat or breathing. For example, I suggest that God's life flows into them with each breath they take. I allow them half a dozen breaths in order to make the connection and foster the awareness.

Having children relax and become more aware of God are easier than getting children to be open and trusting of each other. To facilitate openness, I might use a parable of a clam on the seashore as a way of moving from relaxation to openness. "Go digging for clams in your imagination," I suggest. "Notice a clam will not open up when there's noise around or when somebody pokes at it and disturbs it. But if you stand back and get very quiet so the clam is no longer afraid, it takes a little peek and slowly opens, bit by bit. A snail does the same thing," I add. "If it's afraid it stays locked inside. Our opening prayer is like a clam or a snail asking to be free and without fear to respond to the Spirit. You are like clams. Once you open up, you become vulnerable and open to God. You can also be open to others. Ask God to help you not to be afraid of what you see and what others see. Ask to be free to share and to understand what others share."

Once children are relaxed and centered, that is, aware of

God and trusting, you can suggest some meditative focus, get their imaginations started on the topic, and invite them to let their feelings flow in response to the music you play.

Can You Let a Group of Children Create Their Own Personal Meditations?

Actually, even when you suggest a focus for a group, each child in the group creates his or her own personal experience together with God. So in a very true sense children are always creating their own meditations.

However, you can introduce a group of children into a meditation that is almost completely spontaneous and open-ended, for example, by suggesting that the children meditate on a special feeling they may be feeling right now and simply talk to Jesus about it. If your children are relaxed and open, even such a simple suggestion will be enough to release a meditative atmosphere in the group.

CHAPTER **9**

Meditation Step by Step

If I were a parent or teacher reading this book, what I'd like to see right now is a step-by-step method telling me how to help children meditate. I realize that the deepest moments of meditation and contemplation are really an interpersonal encounter with God which no human can program ahead of time. And for those precious moments there is no formula. But in the important preparatory moments before this encounter we can program what happens in such a way that the child's encounter with God is enhanced.

One method which has proved effective for over four hundred years is the method of St. Ignatius Loyola, the founder of the Jesuits. His manual for spiritual growth, called *The Spiritual Exercises,* contains a basic three-stage formula for meditation and contemplation: (1) getting ready, (2) meditating, and (3) reviewing. The meditation method I have been presenting throughout this book is essentially that of Ignatius. Each of the meditations in Part III have been developed in detail following the Ignatian style.

PREPARATION ELEMENTS

Getting ready for meditation usually includes four steps: (1) awareness of the presence of God, (2) relaxation and centering, (3) history and focus of meditation theme, and (4) asking for the grace you need.

These four basic preparation steps may be presented in almost any order or variety. A meditation will usually be successful if you include most of them.

They are offered as a set of suggestions, a guideline, not as rigid rules. They are meant to help, not hinder you. Your personal way of doing the four elements makes each experience unique. When you visit a friend you usually have a certain set of things you do, but you do them without slavishly following a ritual order. In this sense, then, these suggestions are given not to bind you but to set you free to be creative in the Lord with the children given to your care.

All of the preparation elements have already been discussed, so I need not do that again here, except to make a few comments about each one.

Regarding awareness of God's presence, I often find it helpful to associate this awareness with something tangible, like making the Sign of the Cross, inhaling one's breath, holding grandma's blanket, lighting a special candle, or stepping inside a church. In each case, a physical symbol acts as a reminder to the child of a spiritual, unseen reality. Each child will usually show a preference for a particular symbol of God's presence, so find these preferences and use them.

Relaxation and centering may take time to learn at first, but with practice they become easier and easier as well as more and more enjoyable and attractive. As I suggested previously, centering may be combined with awareness of the presence of God.

Sometimes history and focus of meditation is more important than at other times. History refers to the background of the meditative topic. For example, when focusing on the birth of Jesus in Bethlehem, it might be important for some children to know why Mary and Joseph left Nazareth, why they came to Bethlehem, how Jesus came to be born in a stable, and so on. Children tend to plunge into the meditative flow when the topic or theme is clearly and precisely focused. For example, it is too diffuse to suggest to children simply to meditate on Jesus' birth. It would be much more focused to meditate on how Mary holds Jesus and what she says to him, on what Jesus' face looks like and how he moves his body, or what gifts the visitors brought to Jesus.

In choosing a focus, select a topic that will interest children at their own level of intellectual, emotional, and interpersonal development. For example, if your children value friendship, focus on being a friend of Jesus; if they are interested in sports or physical activity, focus on Jesus' physical activity; if they are interested in showing care and affection, let them display their feelings toward Jesus. For some children you may find it helpful to paraphrase the biblical reading in order better to engage their inner senses and evoke their affective responses. Remember, the objective in meditation is primarily to open hearts rather than to engage logical, historical, or scientific minds.

Give meditating children only enough historical background to make the theme understandable and realistic, since children are not usually interested in history for the sake of history.

Asking for the grace you need is a special Ignatian element in meditation, an additional way of focusing your meditation. By asking for a specific grace—knowing Jesus better, loving Jesus more, following Jesus in his way of serving others, growing in faith, overcoming jealousy, discovering joy—you make a choice and agree to use your energy in making your choice come true. It's like going to visit a friend with the explicit intention of asking for a favor; you don't forget about the favor you want since it is your primary reason for making a visit. Similarly, when you come to meditation with a specific wish or desire, your attention and interest in the meditation are usually intensified because of the favor that you want from God, and thus your meditation is enhanced. Asking for a grace also reminds children to become aware of what they need to grow as sons and daughters of God. Although it is not absolutely essential to have children ask for a specific grace each time they meditate, I feel sure that doing so will profit their growth in spirit.

DURING THE MEDITATION

During the body of a meditation, Ignatius presents two major elements.

The Meditation Proper
Opening the inner self to meditation and contemplation
Colloquy: having a heart-to-heart conversation with the Father or Jesus

Again, these elements need not be separated or performed in this order. Rather, Ignatius feels that both these actions are a part of the encounter with God to which humans can contribute.

Ignatius also suggests that you allow your affection toward the holy family to surface. Speak to them, especially of your joy, love, and gratitude to God for sending his son to be our brother and redeemer. Such expressions of faith and affection flowing from the interaction between you and the characters in the biblical story are called by Ignatius a colloquy. For Ignatius, the colloquy is an essential element in any meditation or contemplation. This loving exchange between creator and creature marks a high point in the God-human relationship, a sacred moment possible to humans most uniquely in this kind of prayer.

I encourage children in meditation both to *listen* to God's communication—which may come in images, feelings, bodily responses, and inner sensory experience—and to *speak* to God in the same ways, that is, not only with words and sentences but with images, feelings, bodily responses, and inner sensory experiences. Thus, both God and child use the child's body, mind, and spirit as the very medium of interpersonal exchange. In a word, the God encounter happens in the child's whole person. The colloquy is an expression of this loving interaction.

It is very important to remember and to communicate the following to children who meditate: The meditation, which takes place in your inner world, remains incomplete until its gifts, graces, and insights are (1) consciously acknowledged, and (2) carried back to your outer world in order to transform that world in some way toward the kingdom of God.

The ultimate objective in Christian meditation is always to help bring about the kingdom of God, or, in another metaphor, to help build the total Body of Christ. When meditation is used merely to make the meditator feel good, it remains incomplete. It is God's wish that children in meditation be gifted with a sense of joy, peace, love, and faith, and it is never wrong to encourage these gifts in children. And perhaps it is well in the beginnings of meditation to encourage children to delight in the good feelings meditation brings, for in this way they nurture an attraction to meditation. However, parents and teachers should eventually encourage children to observe how their good feelings can have a positive effect on others, how they are better able to relax, to deal with pain and disappointments, or to play with their friends with less fighting and jealousy than they used to. While some children will make the connection between their meditation and their improved attitudes toward themselves and others, other children may need to have it pointed out.

This transformation of gifts and energy given in meditation to energy and gifts for the outer world begins in the reflection period after meditation. Reflection questions that the guide may suggest to meditators usually begin with: "What happened to you during meditation?" "What did you discover about yourself? About God? About other people?"

"What kind of gifts, energies and awarenesses did you receive in meditation?"

Once children have brought to speech some answers and realizations, you may ask further questions which make the link to the outer world concretely practical, for example, "Is there someone with whom you would like to share the love God has for you?" "Whom do you know who needs those same gifts and awarenesses?" "How could you bring what you learned in meditation into your life at home? At school? Among your friends?"

Let children struggle to answer such questions by themselves even if it takes many weeks or months for them to discover how they can connect their meditation world with their outer world. Adults will be tempted to *tell* children what they *should* do. Of course, adults may suggest some options; that is not harmful, for sometimes children need a hint or a suggestion. What children do not need are explicit directions. You will know you are trying to direct children when your comments are given in terms of, "You should . . ." or "You must . . ." or "You ought . . ." or, more subtly, "Don't you think it would be nice if you . . ." Instead, help each child struggle with the unique call God is giving to this child at this time. That is your final challenge as a guide.

A Summary of Steps in Meditation

The three stages of the meditation experience may be summarized as follows.

The Stages of Meditation
Stage One: Getting Ready
1. Relaxation: Let your body enjoy being comfortably involved.
2. Centering: Let your spirit be aware of God's presence within you.

3. Theme: Let your mind focus on the topic of your meditation.
4. Scripture: Read or tell the necessary parts of the story.
5. Petition: Ask God for what you need today.
Stage Two: Meditating
6. Meditation (with music): Let your imagination and
feelings get into the theme.
7. Ending: Thank Jesus for the meditation when you are
finished.
Stage Three: Reviewing
8. Review: Talk over, with others if possible, the gifts and
insights you received during the experience and how
you might share them in your everyday world.

The intent of the guide during *preparation* is to lead children from the outer world to the gateway of the inner world
where God may be met person to person.

The intent of the guide during the *meditation* itself is to
keep children in the flow, inviting them to go as deeply as
they are capable into interaction with the spiritual forces of
God.

The intent of the guide during *review* is to help children
bring back the treasures they found in the inner world for use
in transforming their outer world, so that in the end neither
the children nor their world remain the same. They are
slowly being transformed by Christ into the Total Christ.

CHAPTER 10

Creating Your Own Meditations with Music

I hope the following list of musical suggestions gives you some direction in choosing meditation music for your children. In my meditation work, I have found these pieces useful among children five years of age and older. If you don't have access to any of these recordings, you will probably have to find your own music—which is what I prefer to do anyway.

The basic principle in choosing music selections for meditation with children is this: *If the selection's mood continually supports a meditation's desired mood, that music selection will probably help children meditate.*

I find that musical selections which change mood frequently or abruptly are usually not helpful for meditation. Sometimes, however, when you need only five minutes of, say, gentle music, you can excerpt a five-minute gentle portion from a longer, varied piece. In such cases, I prefer to make a cassette recording beforehand of the exact portion of the piece I want to use for meditation.

I also find it a good rule before using any musical selection for meditation with children to test it on myself and my children (who are now seasoned meditators). In this way, I use only music I know is effective with a group. When testing new music, remember to let yourself grow relaxed and centered before you listen, since music seems to produce effects different in those deeply relaxed from those busy and listening on the run.

In this list of recordings, simply because of a lack of space, I have not included selections from pop, standard, jazz, rock, folk, choral, or electronic music, although I have effectively used many individual selections in these genres to foster meditation and contemplation in children.

Recordings marked with an asterisk I have found to be extremely versatile and successful with children.

MUSIC FOR MEDITATION WITH CHILDREN

Composer and Selection	Mood
Bach, *Brandenburg Concerto* #2	ornate but gentle
Barber, *Adagio for Strings*	spiritual, awe
Bax, *The Garden of Fand*	fairy tale feeling
Beethoven, *Symphony* #6 (Pastoral) side one	excellent for country scenes
Brahms, *Symphony* #1, 3rd movement	tranquil, graceful
Britten, *A Simple Symphony,* Op.4	many short dramatic elements
Canteloube, *Songs of the Auvergne*	gentle, supportive
Los Chacos, *El Condor Pasa/La Flute Magique*	merry, exciting
Chopin, *Nocturne in E Flat Major,* Op. 9	poignant
Chopin, *Concerto in F Minor,* No. 2	strong, yet gentle
°Copland, *Appalachian Spring*	wide variety of moods
Debussy, *Dances Sacrée et Profane*	many moods to choose
Debussy, "Sunken Cathedral"	robust, solemn
°Delius, *In a Summer Garden*	excellent potpourri of emotions to choose from
Environments, "The Psychologically Ultimate Seashore"	natural sounds
°Glazunov, *The Seasons,* Ballet, Op. 67	seasonal imagery

Greig, *Peer Gynt Suites* 1 *and* 2	lilting, bouncy
*Grofe, *Grand Canyon Suite*	sometimes serene, sometimes exhilarating
*Holst, *The Planets*	warm, flowing
Liszt, *Liebestraum*	dreamy
Rachmaninoff, *Piano Concerto* #2	sometimes triumphant and martial, sometimes quiet and sentimental
Ravel, *Daphnis and Chloe*, Suite #2	excellent for beginning imagery
*Respighi, *Pines of Rome, Fountains of Rome*	nature imagery
Rimsky-Korsakoff, *Scheherazade*	wide range of moods
Rodrigo, *Concierto de Aranjuez*, 2nd movement	gentle and pensive
Rossini, Overture to *La Gazza Ladra*	humor and irony
Sibelius, *The Swan of Tuonela*	sad and sentimental
Sinding, *Rustle of Spring*	bright and alive
Smetana, *Ma Vlast* ("The High Castle")	awesome structure
Smetana, *Moldau*	gentle, flowing
Tarrega, *Recuerdos de la Alhambra*	pensive, evocative
Tchaikovsky, *The Nutcracker Suite*, "Waltz of the Flowers"	delicate, graceful
Vaughn Williams, *Fantasia on Greensleeves*	warm, human relationships
Vivaldi, *The Four Seasons, Winter*	active release of feelings

BACKGROUND RESOURCE MATERIAL

Books

Anderson, Marianne and Savary, Louis. *Passages: A Guide for Pilgrims of the Mind*. New York: Harper & Row, 1972.

Bonny, Helen and Savary, Louis. *Music and Your Mind: Listening With a New Consciousness*. Baltimore: ICM Press.

Rozman, Deborah. *Children and Meditation*.

Savary, Louis. *Creativity in Children: Stimulating Imaginative Responses to Music*. Baltimore: ICM Press, 1974.

Savary, Louis and Ehlen-Miller, Margaret. *Mindways: A Guide for Exploring Your Mind*. New York: Harper & Row, 1978.

Recordings and Cassettes
Louis Savary narrates 3 LPs:
   Creative Listening, Vol. I

Creative Listening, Vol. II
Opening the Bible, the First Books
    All published by ICM Press, Baltimore, Md.
Theresa Scheihing narrates *Meeting Jesus: Meditation with Music for Children*, NCR Cassettes, 1980.
Louis Savary narrates *The Inner Me*, NCR Cassettes, 1978.

MEDITATION THEMES FOR DIFFERENT CHILDHOOD AGES

Children at different ages are attracted to different themes for meditation, or at least to different emphases. In the early years, for example, children are always talking about play, but to adolescents the word play sounds very childish. As children grow and develop, their interests and needs change. The motivation to meditate seems strongest when meditation themes correspond to personal developmental patterns. I want to share with you some areas of special interest or preoccupation consistently found among children according to their age level. These notes, which reflect children's personal development during six different stages, may give you ideas for developing additional meditative material for your children.

PRESCHOOL YEARS (GENERALLY AGES 3–5)

Children here are preoccupied with their bodies, bodily functions, and needs. Hence, meditations involving movement, gesture, mime, procession, ritual, and dance seem appropriate at this age. Meditations containing elements of laughter, shouting, running, eating, hiding, and the like will prove attractive. Since children at this age are developing their emotional expression, they appreciate opportunities to test the limits of their affectivity in a safe atmosphere. At the pre-school level there is also a budding consciousness of one's power, energy, and identity, so meditations which build on these themes are usually attractive to the preschooler.

Early School Years (generally ages 5–7)

Preoccupation with one's body continues at this stage, as well as awareness of one's own strength and unique identity. Encourage and respect that uniqueness whenever you can. During these years the simple play of earlier years becomes "the business of living," and life roles are endlessly rehearsed with playmates. Children here like to step in and out of the shoes of others, especially those of adults who populate their daily lives. At this age imaginary friends are prominent too, so it is easy to introduce spiritual guardians, Jesus as friend, fellowship with the saints.

Chum Period (generally ages 7–12)

During the chum years children develop a capacity to care and empathize. They know a reverence for life. It is the age for wanting pets. Themes of caring for others, especially animals, and the earth—planting, growing, nurturing, protecting, ecology—can be powerful in meditation. Children here are usually models of companionship and cooperation; they are true friends, "comrades in arms" willing to share good times and bad times together. They wish to become mature adults, yet they fear growing up. For the first time, children at this age can grasp the experience of death and loss. All of these themes offer rich meditative material.

Junior High Period (generally ages 12–14)

During this period daydream capacities may be capitalized upon. Girls tend to fantasize about relationships, while boys tend to fantasize about projects, i.e., doing things. Children at this time begin choosing their life values and in doing so begin exploring in fantasy different spheres of life—family, school, peers, leisure, religion—trying to value each sphere separately and also to integrate what they value. Meditation themes which help put the world together and find a place for "me" in it are usually attractive to those of junior high age.

ADOLESCENT PERIOD (GENERALLY AGES 14–16)

This is for most young people a period of tensions—sexual, social, emotional. Adolescents are watching themselves change, discovering their potential, and doing their first real shaping of adult identity. Since key themes for them at this time are acceptance and rejection, meditations which help foster self-acceptance are a welcome relief to beleaguered adolescents. Meditations which deal gently and lovingly with their rejections, fears, and failures are also needed.

MATURING PERIOD (GENERALLY 18 YEARS OR OLDER)

Meditation for this age group may introduce themes of personal commitment, social responsibility, freedom, mature relationships, and the discipline involved in shaping personal identity.

I hope that you enjoy creating meditations with music for your children as much as I do for mine. How nice it is to invite children into a relationship with God and each other in such a comfortably joyful way.

Part Three

MEDITATIONS:
THROUGH THE
LITURGICAL YEAR

CHAPTER **11**

Meditations for Advent

Each meditation for children in these ten chapters follows the structure "Getting Ready, Meditating, and Reviewing" on page 93. Each chapter contains five meditations on a single theme. I used each set of five with my class as a week of meditations, doing one each day. They may also be used, singly or successively, in other ways as your creativity suggests.

My texts and words are offered as suggestions. I'm simply presenting them here as I might give them to my class. Their language follows my style of speaking. Feel free to adapt these ideas in whatever way feels comfortable to you.

Instead of suggesting specific musical selections for each meditation, I chose simply to suggest a mood that fits the theme. This leaves you free to find music from recordings available to you that seems to create an emotional atmosphere that supports the meditation. You may also want to consult the musical selections listed on pp. 101–2 for additional ideas.

When speaking the words of these meditations to children, use a clear, gentle voice, as if you were telling a bedtime story. Speak slowly and let there be pauses after each image or idea. A meditation is never to be rushed.

1. What Is a Prophet?

Music. Beforehand, select a piece of music that feels hopeful and has an air of expectancy.

Relaxation. If children are their usual active or restless selves, you may want to take a minute or two to ask them to begin letting themselves relax. You might suggest, "Close your eyes and take a few deep breaths, gently and very slowly." Let your voice speak gently and slowly, too. "As you do, you can picture your body relaxing from the top of your head down to your toes. See and feel your muscles growing comfortable and relaxed."

(You may find it helpful to use the same relaxation suggestions for a few subsequent meditations, since repetition usually allows a relaxation procedure to become familiar and natural to a child.)

Centering. "Get your inner sacred place ready for God to come and be with you." (Pause.)

Theme. "This week's theme is Advent, and today's meditation is about a prophet, John the Baptist. Did you know that a prophet is someone who can tell what is going to happen before it actually happens? A prophet prepares people for great events and the coming of important people. If you listen with your inner ears, you may hear something very special about Jesus through the voice of the prophet."

Scripture. Slowly read Luke 3:1-3.

Petition. "Today, let's ask Jesus for a gift for our hearts. Use your own words to say, 'Jesus, help me become a prophet and prepare others to recognize you when you come into their lives.' "

Meditation. "Let the music I play lead you into your meditation." (You may begin music softly at this point.) "If you want some suggestions, you might in your imagination like to follow John the Baptist as he stands along the bank of the Jordan River speaking to you and to all the people who gather around him. Hear John telling about the coming of the Savior, Jesus Christ. What is he saying to you about Jesus?" (Turn music volume up, and let it play for two or three minutes more.)

Ending. "The music is over. Tell God how you are feeling right now, and tell God about what you experienced during your meditation. When you're finished, you may open your eyes and sit up quietly."

Review. Children may want to talk about their meditative experiences: What did John look like? What did Jesus look like? What did John say? What did they do? How did people feel? Was there any message? And so on. The objective is to help children feel relaxed about sharing their prayer experiences and to honor every child's contribution as uniquely valuable.

2. JOHN THE BAPTIST SHOUTING

Music. Hopeful and exciting.

Relaxation. Repeat the previous relaxation suggestions. Remember to allow children sufficient time to get settled and composed.

Centering. "Get your inner sacred place ready for God, for today God comes with excitement and joy." (Pause.)

Theme. "As we continue the theme of Advent, or coming, today's meditation is about John the Baptist shouting for joy. Listen as I read the scripture telling how John shouted as loud as he could, telling all those who would listen to him that the Lord, the Messiash, Jesus Christ was coming. And he warned them to make the crooked paths of their life straight because Jesus would soon be here."

Scripture. Read Luke 3:4.

Petition. "Let's ask Jesus for a gift for our spirits. Use your own words to say, 'Jesus, show me how to shout out joyfully to all my friends that you are coming to them.'"

Meditation. (Begin music softly.) "Perhaps, as the music plays, you would like to think of the most exciting thing you know about Jesus, something you would like to tell everyone in the world. Hear yourself, standing next to John the Baptist, shouting out your message with joy. Then you may want to hear John telling you to make your crooked paths straight, and see yourself making a straight path along the street where you live, getting everyone outside to watch and wait and be ready because Jesus is on his way. Then wait in silence and look for him." (Increase music's volume and let it play for another few minutes.)

Ending. "The music is over. Tell God how you are feeling right now and tell God what happened to you during your meditation. When you're ready, you may open your eyes and sit up quietly."

Review. Invite children to talk about the most exciting thing they know about Jesus, or what path they made straight, or if they saw Jesus. Gently draw out their joy and let it fill the room.

3. THE HILLS AND VALLEYS OF OUR LIVES

Music. Reflective, quiet, lilting.

Relaxation. Offer suggestions to quiet and relax children. Allow enough time for them to get reflective.

Centering. "Prepare your inner sacred place, for today God comes quietly with gifts." (Pause.)

Theme. "We are still in Advent. In today's meditation we go with John the Baptist who will show us in the mountains and valleys the big and little gifts God has given us."

Scripture. Read Luke 3:5.

Petition. "Today let's ask Jesus, 'Help me to accept the highs and lows of my life and to see that all of them are gifts of love from God.' "

Meditation. (Begin music softly.) "Let the music take you for a walk in the hills with John the Baptist. In your imagination trace your finger along the ridge of a mountain top. Notice how your finger goes up to a peak, then down a little to a valley. Then up, across, and down again. It's fun to trace the peaks and valleys of a mountain! Imagine the valleys to be low spots in your life—the sad, unhappy times. Now, to see yourself filling up those valleys, let your finger take you to the peaks of the mountain. Imagine these to be happy, special moments, joyful feelings you've experienced. Go as high up the mountain as you would like and fill all the valleys with "tip-top" feelings. Life is made up of valleys and peaks. Thank God for both." (Turn up music volume.)

Ending. Offer the usual suggestions for closure.

Review. Ask about sad, unhappy moments remembered, then about tip-top moments. Or ask the children to describe times that feel like valleys and times that feel like mountain peaks. Encourage a sense of integration of both highs and lows, and invite a sense of gratitude for the fullness of sadness *and* joy God gives.

4. WINDING ROADS OF MY LIFE

Music. Meandering, walking music.

Relaxation. As usual, please don't forget the relaxation.

Centering. "Start by going inside yourself where you will find a path, the beginning of a winding path. Then wait there. Don't go anywhere on it yet." (Allow a few moments for centering.)

Theme. "We are still in Advent, still preparing for Jesus' coming. How can *you* prepare for the coming? Let John the Baptist show you what he did. First, let's read a verse from the Bible."

Scripture. Read slowly Luke 3:5.

Petition. "As we are about to set out on the road inside us, let us say quietly, 'Jesus, I know you are coming to meet me. Make me ready to see you and receive you.' "

Meditation. (Begin music softly.) "As the music plays, begin to walk on your winding path. You may hold John the Baptist's hand if you wish. Begin to walk the most winding road you have ever been on. Count all the turns. Notice the rough spots, the curves in the road. How many are there? Now stop. Watch how the road begins to straighten out and become smooth. You can look in the distance and see exactly where you are going. Let yourself believe Jesus is coming and the winding road will be made straight and the rough spots will become smooth. You can see somebody coming toward you. It is probably Jesus. Now, go to meet him." (Music up.)

Ending. The usual closure.

Review. Ask about the road, what it looked like, what made it rough. Did John walk with you? Ask if some saw Jesus and what he looked like. Reassure those who did not see Jesus that maybe they needed a longer time, or maybe they will see him next time, or perhaps they saw him in an earlier meditation, or while they didn't see him they may have "felt" his presence inside their hearts. Remember always to be accepting and supportive of every child. You do not know *how* God is revealing himself to this child, but you can be sure that God *is* revealing himself. Your task is to help keep the child open and, if you can, to help the child find out *how* God is revealing himself in this particular moment.

5. SALVATION FOR ALL PEOPLE

Music. Create a sense of the gathering of many people: use music with strong and confident—even triumphant—feelings.

Relaxation. As usual.

Centering. "Find your way into the quiet center of your self where God is waiting in joy for you."

Theme. "Today we focus on the shared joy that everyone feels about Jesus' coming. We are not alone in our joy, but people all over the earth join us in the sure feeling that Christ is coming."

Scripture. "The Bible says, 'And all mankind shall see the salvation of God' " (Luke 3:6).

Petition. "Let's ask Jesus for understanding. You might say, 'Jesus, who do you want me to tell about you today?' "

Meditation. (Music softly.) "Let's begin our meditation by reviewing the other Advent meditations we made. Become a prophet again like John the Baptist. Once again hear yourself shouting to all your friends that Christ is coming: 'Prepare a way for the Lord.' Next, see the valleys of your life filled with hilltops—the joyful peaks. Next, walk along the winding roads of your life and begin to make them straight. Watch the rough spots, the painful times, begin to feel better, begin to heal. Now listen to the voices of all your friends—all who will listen—joining with you as you walk together singing, 'Christ is coming! Christ is coming! Christ is coming to me!' Prepare." (Music up.)

Ending. The usual closure.

Review. Ask especially about the different friends or people who joined the walk. Emphasize the sense of fellowship followers of Jesus feel with each other.

In review sessions, children's responses may be very concrete. For example, children may prefer to discuss not the winding roads in their heart, but those roads in the area where they live. You may show on a road map how roads actually wind. Similarly, children may choose to discuss mountains or valleys they have seen or hiked over rather than imaginary ones. These are appropriate and acceptable meditative responses since children tend to be very concrete and specific.

You may also invite children to draw the scenes—the rivers, mountains, valleys, and crooked roads—they pictured during meditation.

CHAPTER 12

Meditations for Epiphany: The Manifestation of Jesus to the World

1. OPEN HEARTS AND MINDS

Music. Feelings of longing, openness, seeking.

Relaxation. Use any form of relaxation you find helpful in the situation. Unless children are used to relaxing or already know a method for relaxing, you will want to offer concrete suggestions on *how* to relax, for example, involving breathing and imagination. It is not sufficient simply to order children to relax, since no one can relax on command. Relaxation is not merely a physical state, but involves a certain attitude as well.

Centering. "Prepare your inner sacred place for God to come and be with you." (Pause.)

Theme. "The theme for this season is Epiphany, the manifestation of Jesus to the world. Today we learn to be like the wise men from the East who searched for Jesus with open minds and hearts as they followed a special star."

Scripture. Read slowly Matthew 2:9-10.

Petition. "In asking Jesus for a gift, say something like, 'Jesus, let me shine brightly like the star in the East, leading others to you.'"

117

Meditation. (Music softly.) "Follow the star in your imagination as you begin your journey to Bethlehem with the three wise men to find the Christ Child. Notice the gifts they are bringing to him. Would you like to bring a gift to Jesus? Think of something that is most precious, most valuable to your heart. A gift from your heart would surely please Jesus. The wise men had open minds and hearts because they were longing for the Messiah, waiting and looking for signs of his coming. You may want to think of one thing you will do today that will be like the star, leading you closer to Jesus." (Music volume up.)

Ending. "The music is over. Tell God how you are feeling now and what happened in your meditation. When you're ready, you may open your eyes and sit up quietly."

Review. Children may like to wonder about the gifts the wise men had, the camels they rode, or the children's own gifts. They may find it a little more difficult to say how they will be like a star today, so you may have to help them with that. Older children may be able to describe what the metaphor "open mind and heart" means to them.

2. THE GIFTS OF GOLD

Music. Reflective, quiet, light.

Relaxation. Use whatever way you find effective.

Centering. The usual.

Theme. "Today's theme is the gift of gold which the wise men brought to Jesus. Let us think about gold, one of the most valuable and precious gifts one could give. When we think of what is more precious in our lives, we think of people who are valuable and important to us."

Scripture. Matt. 2:11. It may not be necessary to read aloud the biblical verse for this meditation.

Petition. "Let's ask Jesus to help us recognize and appreciate the preciousness of other people."

Meditation. (Music softly.) "Let's picture pieces of gold in a beautiful cloth purse, and let each piece of gold symbolize and represent a precious person in your life. Touch each piece of gold and as you do quietly say the name of someone important to you—your parents, family, relatives, friends. Now offer to Jesus, along with the wise man's gold, your precious gift of all the people you love, those who have touched your life and made it richer and more beautiful." (Music up.)

Ending. As usual.

Review. Ask children about the gold pieces, how many there were, and what people the gold pieces represented to them. Be accepting of all responses and say "thanks" to each child who shares some meditative experience. You might also like to show children some real gold, discuss the price of gold, emphasize its symbolic value to people, especially at times when people exchange gifts of love.

3. THE GIFT OF FRANKINCENSE

Music. Delicate and beautiful.

Relaxation. Use a gentle way of relaxing here, perhaps one which focuses on breathing. You may even wish to light incense for children to smell.

Centering. "Use your breath to inhale God's life into every part of your being."

Theme. "The wise men brought Jesus another special gift called frankincense. Notice that the last half of the word frankincense is incense. It is a fine, sweet powder and a symbol of reverence. When frankincense burns, it tells you that this is a special, holy place, a place of respect and reverence."

Scripture. Matt. 2:11.

Petition. "Let's ask Jesus to teach us new ways of showing respect for others."

Meditation. (Music softly.) "Watch the wise men lighting this delicate powder and begin to smell the whole room being filled with the sweetest fragrance you can imagine. Frankincense is a special incense used for kings and royalty. It is used only at very special times. Now is special. Join the three wise men and bow down before the Christ Child as you tell him you love him and believe he is the Son of God, the king who has come into our world to bring peace to all people."

Ending. As usual.

Review. Talk about Jesus and what children may have said to him or felt about him. Talk about the Magi. Talk about smells and different incense. You may also want to make the connection with incense used in the church sanctuary at solemn times.

4. THE GIFT OF MYRRH

Music. Suggestions of earth and its seasons, gentle, pastoral.

Relaxation. Any form you like.

Centering. As usual.

Theme. "We are still meditating on the gifts of the wise men. Their third gift to Jesus is a valuable substance, myrrh. Myrrh is a sweet-smelling syrup that flows from certain trees and shrubs that grow in Arabia and Africa. Myrrh is a symbol of saving and caring for all the good things of the earth."

Scripture. Matt. 2:11.

Petition. "Let's ask Jesus for a gift now: 'Jesus, help us take care of all the natural gifts you have made for us.'"

Meditation. (Music softly.) "In your imagination collect some of your favorite 'earth gifts' God has made for you to use, enjoy, and save. The gifts can be things like rocks, trees, or water from the sea. Gather together these bits of natural beauty and offer them with the wise men's myrrh to Jesus as a gift." (Music volume up.)

Ending. Usual ending.

Review. Ask children to tell all the different earth things they would save and bring as gifts to Jesus. Many children may choose similar gifts, and that's okay. (If you are able, bring for showing some sap from a tree so the children may touch and smell it.)

5. THE GIFT OF YOURSELF

Music. Confident, strong music for a journey.

Relaxation. Use your children's favorite method for relaxing.

Centering. "Go inside your heart to the place where you can sense the child Jesus present and the three wise men with him."

Theme. "The word *epiphany* means to show forth, to manifest. Jesus came to invite all people to share in the kingdom of his Father. You are special to Jesus. Each person you ever see is loved by Jesus. The wise men represent you and everyone who journeys with Christ to the Father's heavenly kingdom."

Scripture. Matt. 2:9-11.

Petition. "Let us ask for the grace to be able to say to Jesus: 'Jesus, take all of me. That's the best I have to give you.'"

Meditation. (Music softly.) "Keep your eyes on the star that led you to Bethlehem with the wise men. Look at it and notice how it shines brighter and brighter as it guides you to the continual discovery of Jesus in your everyday life when you offer the most precious gift you have to give, the beautiful gift of yourself." (Music louder.)

Ending. Usual ending.

Review. Begin by talking about the star and how it may have looked to each child, and ask how they might go about offering themselves and their daily activities as a gift to Jesus or the Father. You may have to give samples of such offering from your own life to get the children started.

CHAPTER **13**

Meditations on the Days
of Holy Week

1. PALM SUNDAY: THE BEGINNING OF HOLY WEEK

Music. Parade music full of excitement.

Relaxation. Here it will be well to use simple forms of standing and stretching arms and legs. It might help to have children imagine they are holding and waving palm branches.

Centering. Invite children to let joy bubble up from their center, to let the word "hosanna" (which means "Praise God") be heard resounding inside them, wanting to come out of them and be heard in the world.

Theme. "Palm Sunday marks the beginning of Holy Week. We will walk with Jesus this week to experience the events of his life in our lives today. We will see the many ways people treat their king. Today they celebrate him and create a parade for him, and you may walk next to Jesus who rides on a donkey into the great city of Jerusalem."

Scripture. John 12:12-19

Petition. "Jesus, be the king of my heart and the parade of my life. Let me praise you."

Meditation. (Begin music softly.) "Imagine yourself in a

crowd of people cheering for your favorite person, Jesus. See yourself as part of the large parade of people gathering together to make Jesus their king. Jesus is riding on a donkey. You are standing next to him. Feel others pressing near, for everyone wants to get close to Jesus. Hear yourself cheering and shouting out, 'Hosanna, Jesus. You are my king, king of the whole world.' Imagine waving a palm branch. Touch Jesus with it and look into his eyes as you shout your hosannas. Maybe he will let you ride on the donkey with him, if you want to. It seems as if everyone in the parade wants to be known as a friend and follower of Jesus. Let yourself feel how happy and proud you are knowing you are loved by Jesus, your king." (Music up.)

Ending. "Tell God how much you love Jesus and how happy you are to have him as your friend and king. When you have finished, open your eyes and smile."

Review. Begin with questions of imagery and detail: How many people were there? How were they dressed? Did you have a palm branch? What did Jesus' donkey look like? Was Jesus happy being there? Ask them how they might bring their joy into their everyday lives.

2. PREPARATION FOR PASSOVER: SHALOM

Music. Let there be sounds of festivities and the excitement of getting ready for a celebration dinner.

Relaxation. Use a form of physical movement to relax the children, perhaps lifting feet up and down as if walking, and turning the head this way and that as if looking at different foods in a marketplace.

Centering. "Be conscious of God alive inside of you, filling you with excitement at a celebration with Jesus and his friends."

Theme. "Every year Jewish people have an anniversary dinner party called the passover meal. It is the biggest celebration of the year in memory of the gift of freedom of entering the Promised Land. Think of the times when you helped your family prepare the turkey, cranberry sauce and pumpkin pie for your Thanksgiving dinner. Like Thanksgiving, the Passover is a sacred family time when people are very close to each other and to God. In this meditation you will help Peter and John prepare the Passover dinner."

Scripture. Luke 22:7-13.

Petition. "Let's ask for the gift we want today, saying, 'Jesus, help me take part in preparing our sacred family celebrations.'"

Meditation. (Music softly.) "Imagine yourself with Peter and John as Jesus gives them instructions for getting the Passover meal ready. Hear Jesus say, 'You will need to buy a lamb, some good wine, unleavened bread, and some herbs.' As you walk with the apostles, see yourself meeting a man carrying a jar of water. Follow him as he leads you to a house and shows you a large furnished room, where you can get the meal ready. Imagine you are setting the table, arranging the seats so everyone will fit. Then picture yourself preparing the meal from the food you bought. Imagine you are placing the bread and the cup of wine where Jesus will be sitting. Now choose where you would like to sit. As you look around you can see that all is ready. Let yourself realize that this is not going to be an ordinary meal, but Jesus will give us something special at this meal." (Music up.)

Ending. "Talk to Jesus and thank him for inviting you to this special meal and for letting you help with the preparation. Tell him how you are enjoying yourself."

Review. Discuss sensory details. Ask, for example, how the upper room looked, what food they bought, what they did to prepare it, where they sat at the table, who else was there, and so on. Ask about their feelings and what parts of the meditation they most enjoyed. Inquire how they might do similar things at their own family celebrations.

3. WASHING OF FEET: GO AND DO LIKEWISE

Music. Use a selection that emphasizes a mood of tenderness and caring.

Relaxation. Let the relaxation focus on the feet and legs. Perhaps the children could be seated. Ask them to concentrate on their legs, feet and toes.

Centering. "Imagine God is present in the room. God is everywhere, but especially during this meditation think of God's love like the air in the room, and be especially conscious of the air surrounding your feet. Let yourself feel God touching your feet."

Theme. "Everyone has arrived for the dinner party. Look around and see them. Imagine you are there with Jesus and the apostles. In a moment we will see Jesus give us an example of the way we should treat others."

Scripture. John 13:4-15. Perhaps it might be more helpful for you to paraphrase the biblical passage for the children; you may use your own version or follow my suggestions below.

Petition. "Let's all ask Jesus for a gift with the words, 'Jesus, show me ways to follow your example of serving others.' "

Meditation. (Music softly.) "Imagine Jesus taking off his outer robe and tying a towel around his waist. Can you guess what Jesus is going to do? Watch him pour some water into a wash basin and begin to wash the apostles' feet and dry them with his towel. You can see by the expression on their faces that the disciples are very surprised. You can hear them telling each other that they should be washing Jesus' feet, instead of Jesus washing theirs. Hear them also asking each other, 'Why is Jesus doing this to us?' And now imagine it is your turn. See

Jesus kneeling in front of you washing and drying your feet. You can feel just by the way Jesus touches you that he cares very much for you. Look into his eyes and hear him tell you he is serving you because he loves you. And he wants you to serve others, to be aware of the needs of others, and to follow his example of gentle kindness." (Music up.)

Ending. "Tell Jesus you can feel how much he loves you, and how you want to help others as Jesus helps you."

Review. Ask about feelings: How did the apostles feel about getting their feet washed? How did you feel about getting your feet washed? In what ways can you be kind to others? Perhaps a few children will have stories of their own care for other children, their parents, or their pets. Invite sharing of these stories. Perhaps you can be first to tell such a story, to give children a clear sense of what you are asking for.

4. THE LORD'S SUPPER: BREAKING OF THE BREAD

Music. Use a selection that creates a mood of sacred stillness. Barber's *Adagio for Strings* works well here.

Relaxation. Use a procedure that does not emphasize physical movement. Rather focus on breathing or heart beat, bringing about a sense of stillness.

Centering. Use a centering procedure that focuses on God's presence in the heart and the child's hunger for spiritual food.

Theme. "After Jesus washed the feet of his apostles and returned to his place at the table, a sense of stillness and expectancy filled the room because everyone began to realize something special was happening. Every word and gesture of Jesus would be important. You might remember a time when someone very close to you waited to give you an important message. You could sense the special emotion in your body by the way they looked and talked and acted. They were silent before they spoke. Jesus is like this now, and the specialness has something to do with the bread and wine in front of him.

Scripture. Luke 22:14-20.

Petition. "Let's ask Jesus for the gift we want, saying to him, 'Jesus, I believe the food you give us is really your body and blood.'"

Meditation. (Music softly.) "Imagine you and all the apostles are looking very intently at Jesus. You are waiting eagerly. And wondering. Now hear the voice of Jesus full of love and warmth saying, 'I have wanted very much to eat this passover meal with you before I suffer.' Then watch as Jesus takes the bread into his hands, thanks his Father, breaks the bread into pieces, and gives it to his disciples, saying, 'This is my body which shall be broken for you.' Then see him take the cup of wine into his hands, thank God, and say to his friends, 'Take and drink this, for this is the cup of my blood.' Then hear him tell his apostles, 'Do this in memory of me.' This food and drink is Jesus himself. As you picture yourself receiving the bread and wine, speak to Jesus from your heart." (Music up.)

Ending. "Thank Jesus for inviting you to this first communion service and tell him you believe you are filled with his life."

Review. Ask about the details of the communion: What did the bread look like? How did it taste? What did the cup look like? What color was the wine? How did it taste? How was this experience like holy communion in church? How was it different? Suggest they might relive this meditation the next time they are present for the Eucharist.

5. DEATH: RESURRECTION

Music. Selections for meditation on Jesus' suffering and death on the cross.

Relaxation. If children are open to it, ask them to stand with arms outstretched as Jesus did on the cross. As they stand this way, ask them to be aware of the sensations in their arms and to stay concentrated on their arms.

Centering. "Let yourself imagine Jesus' arms becoming your arms and your arms becoming Jesus' arms. Let his body become your body; his head, your head; his heart, your heart. Let yourself feel Jesus' whole body in your body and your body in his body. Let yourself feel Jesus' life joining your life so that you are experiencing his life and your life at the same time."

Theme. "Jesus has spent his life on earth preparing for this moment—his death and resurrection—that we might live forever in his Father's kingdom. Jesus' death will not be an ending but a beginning. It is difficult to understand death as a beginning, but yet we ask to believe this because Jesus promises it is so."

Scripture. Luke 23:43-46.

Petition. "Let's ask Jesus for the gift of faith, saying, 'Jesus, help me believe death leads to new life in your Father's kingdom.'"

Meditation. (Music softly.) "Have you ever experienced the death of someone you loved, someone who was close to you—a family member, a friend, or a pet? When they died it seemed as if they were gone forever, didn't it? With Jesus it is different. Listen to the voice of Jesus as he talks to the good thief hanging on a cross next to him. Jesus says, 'This day you shall be with me in paradise.' Look at the face of the thief after he heard these words of Jesus. He is looking at Jesus hanging in pain and close to death. The good thief believed he would share eternal life with Jesus in his Father's kingdom. You may talk with Jesus and the good thief about death and how it can be the beginning of life to those who believe in Jesus." (Music up.)

Ending. "Thank Jesus for the gift of his life and the promise he makes to you that you will live forever with him."

Review. Ask about death experiences the children may have shared. Ask how it felt to watch Jesus die, or what they might have said to Jesus if they were the good thief. They may also enjoy sharing what they imagine life in the Father's kingdom might be like.

CHAPTER 14

Meditations for Easter: Recognizing Jesus in Our Lives

1. WALKING TO EMMAUS

Music. Casual, relaxed, pastoral.

Relaxation. A variation in relaxation procedures may help here, for example, using some forms of stretching or very slow physical movement. Relaxation is intensified through concentration, by asking children to focus on their muscles and to concentrate on the feelings in moving parts of their bodies. You might say, "Notice how the muscles of your arms feel as you move them slowly up above your head. Now, see how they feel as you very slowly let them float downward toward the floor."

Centering. "Open your whole body, mind, and spirit so that God can come and fill you with joy and light."

Theme. "Today's meditation begins with a scene that happened on the first Easter day. Think of a time when you walked in the countryside, and imagine yourself walking along the road to Emmaus with two disciples. They are talking about Jesus and all the events that have taken place since Good Friday. Notice that they are sad and confused and wondering about many things."

Scripture. Luke 24:13-14.

131

Petition. "Ask Jesus for a special gift in words like, 'Jesus, help me accept with faith what is difficult for me to understand about you.'"

Meditation. (Music softly.) "As you walk with these two disciples of Jesus, listen to what they are saying. They are asking many questions. 'Is it true?' they wonder. 'Can we really believe this has happened? Can it be that Jesus really rose from the dead?' Perhaps you would like to walk and talk with them, asking some questions of your own about Jesus as the music plays." (Music up.)

Ending. "The music is over. Tell God how you are feeling right now, and tell God what happened to you during your meditation. When you're ready, you may open your eyes and sit up quietly."

Review. Invite children to share the questions they asked in the meditation. Perhaps they would like to describe or draw the two disciples and the countryside. They may even be able to share some questions they have about Jesus.

2. JESUS JOINS YOU ON YOUR JOURNEY

Music. Music can have a lighter quality here, but still pastoral.

Relaxation. Use whatever works with your children.

Centering. As usual.

Theme. "As you are walking and talking with the disciples on the road to Emmaus, a man joins you. He seems to know a lot about Jesus and you find yourself very interested in what this man is saying. Who is he?"

Scripture. Luke 24:15-17.

Petition. "Jesus, help me to recognize you in all the ways you show yourself to me each day."

Meditation. (Music softly.) "Look closely at this man who has come and joined your group. Do you recognize him?

What does he look like? Have you ever seen him before? If you like, ask the man his name. You will be very surprised and happy when he tells you." (Music up.)

Ending. Follow the usual formula.

Review. It will be interesting to get children to describe or draw the man who joins them. Don't be surprised if some children recognize and name the man as someone other than Jesus. Don't correct them, but stay with their intuition. Ask them about the feelings they felt when this man came among them.

3. RECOGNIZING JESUS IN THE BREAKING OF THE BREAD

Music. Dinner music with an undercurrent of joy and surprise.

Relaxation. Usual procedure. By now, relaxation should be a habit with your meditating children, so it should take only about a minute to reach a deeply relaxed state.

Centering. The usual.

Theme. "We are still walking with the disciples and the new man on Easter Sunday. You ask him to stay with you a little longer. You really don't want him to leave you just yet. See how you are all seated around a dinner table in the inn."

Scripture. Luke 24:28-32.

Petition. "Jesus, help me believe that you are truly present each time I receive you in holy communion."

Meditation. (Music softly) "You may picture yourself sitting anywhere you wish at the table. You may even bring a friend with you to share this wonderful experience. Now watch how Jesus takes the bread into his hands, blesses it, and gives it to you. And you recognize Jesus in the gift of himself." (Music up.)

Ending. "Close by thanking God in your own way."

Review. Ask children to describe the table scene, who sits where, who says what, and what Jesus looks like. Ask also how it may have felt to be present near Jesus and to receive the holy bread from his hands.

4. TELLING EVERYONE THAT JESUS IS RISEN

Music. Triumphal music.
Relaxation. Some familiar relaxation procedure.
Centering. As usual.
Theme. "This is a meditation for encouraging your spirit to shout with joy using words like, 'Jesus is risen! Alleluia! Jesus is alive! Alleluia!' You want to tell everybody that your friend Jesus is alive and gloriously well."
Scripture. Luke 24:33-35.
Petition. "Jesus, please keep the alleluias of your resurrection always singing in my heart, and help me show others how to sing and tell about you."
Meditation. (Music softly.) "Picture yourself running through the streets with the disciples. And feel how excited you are inside to tell all your friends about your wonderful discovery of Jesus alive! Notice the faces of people you tell and the surprise in their eyes when you say you have walked and talked with the Lord and have shared a meal with him as well as the breaking of bread. It is such a full and overflowing feeling of joy to have for the rest of your life—to tell everyone you know that Jesus is risen, Alleluia!"
Ending. As usual.
Review. Talk about feelings and faces, running and sharing. Underscore the feelings of joy that comes when people know and believe the Lord is risen.

5. KEEPING THE SPIRIT OF JESUS ALIVE

Music. Strong, joyful, even triumphant.
Relaxation. As usual.

Centering. As usual.

Theme. "Jesus lives through his spirit of love in you. He is alive in your friendly smile. He can be heard in your voice when you speak with loving kindness. He is reflected in the way you care about the feelings of others. Jesus lives in you and in every person filled with his spirit."

Scripture. Luke 24:48-49.

Petition. "Jesus, tell me what I need to know to keep the joy of your risen life in my heart."

Meditation. (Music softly.) "See Jesus filling your heart with his love. Now watch his love pour out of you and think of someone you will share Jesus with today. Who will it be? What will you do? Spend some moments as the music plays thinking about the love you have to give." (Music up.)

Ending. As usual.

Review. Invite children to share the people they saw and experienced in their meditation, the people they might tell about Jesus. Ask also about the many different ways (you may even list them on a chalkboard or paper) that Jesus lives through them in a spirit of love. You may have to be the first contributor to the list. For this, you may adapt some examples from the theme section of this meditation.

CHAPTER 15

Meditations on the Ascension of Jesus

1. JESUS GATHERS HIS FRIENDS FOR THE LAST TIME

Music. Gentle, tender music with a hint of sadness.

Relaxation. I suggest using a way of relaxing the children that involves breathing. Help them get in touch through each breath with the life and energy of God quietly filling them. Encourage them to quiet their inner feelings so they can listen to God within them.

Centering. "Please be aware of being one of Jesus' closest friends and let yourself feel his presence in your heart. Feel it in a way that tells you he will never leave you."

Theme. "Sometimes it is very difficult to leave a close friend or someone you love very much. Jesus knew his work on earth was finished and he was preparing to return to his Father in heaven, so he gathered his closest friends around him to say goodbye. He had a going-away message for them."

Scripture. Read Acts 1:6.

Petition. "Let us say to Jesus something like, 'Jesus, quiet all my inside feelings so I can hear you when you speak your message to me.'"

Meditation. (Begin music softly.) "Picture Jesus gathering his closest friends around him to say goodbye. You are one of Jesus' closest friends, so you may stand among his disciples if you wish. How does it feel to know that a close friend of yours will be leaving? Perhaps you can think of a time when you wanted to stay with someone longer, but you had to leave them. Jesus knows how important the time of leaving is, so he wants to leave his friends a message. If you listen with your inner ears you will hear Jesus begin to share a very special going-away message. Be very still and listen as the music plays." (Music up.)

Ending. "The music is over. Tell God how you're feeling right now, and say thanks to God for the special message you may have received. When you're finished doing that, you may open your eyes and sit up quietly."

Review. Encourage children to talk about times they experienced separation in their own lives. Then help them make the connection with the disciples' experience of separation from Jesus. Don't forget to explore the many special messages the children may have received from Jesus. To get the children started, you may wish to share a special message you had from Jesus in doing this meditation.

2. THE PROMISE OF WHAT IS TO COME

Music. A quiet selection with an undercurrent of expectation.

Relaxation. "Use a way to relax that will be best for you today. Take your time. And when you are done, let your body be full of readiness for something unknown to happen." (Allow some moments for children to relax themselves.)

Centering. "Picture God not only filling up your insides but also surrounding you with love. Let yourself be waiting for something, but you don't know what it can be."

Theme. "Did you ever have a feeling something was going to happen but you didn't know when or how it was going to happen? Sometimes it's hard to put such feelings into words. You know you have these feelings but you don't know how you came to have them. That's how it is with heaven. You have a sense heaven will happen but you don't know where or when. That's how the disciples are today, wondering about the unknown."

Scripture. Read Acts 1:7.

Petition. "Let's ask God for a gift using words like, 'Jesus, prepare me to be ready for the unknown, to be open to the promise of what is to come.'"

Meditation. (Music softly.) "Stand with Jesus' disciples and hear Jesus say the Father is in charge of the future and he sets the dates for what is to come. You can hear the disciples asking Jesus when the kingdom would come and whether it would be on the earth. Then hear Jesus say that his Father's kingdom is in heaven and you always have to be prepared because you won't know when it might arrive. Let yourself feel Jesus wants you to be with him and his Father in the kingdom. Feel how exciting it is to know there is a heaven—a kingdom—waiting for you, and yet you don't know when it will happen. Let yourself feel that excitement as the music plays." (Music up.)

Ending. Suggest an ending that involves personal affective expression to God.

Review. Invite children to describe some of their experiences. If there is little response, you might begin by asking them their fantasies of what heaven will be like. Perhaps some children are looking forward to an approaching unknown experience in their own lives and might want to talk about it.

3. BEING WITNESSES

Music. Find a gentle selection whose theme stretches one's awareness to wider worlds.

Relaxation. Perhaps some physical stretching of arms and legs to symbolize the length and breadth of the planet earth. Ask children to feel the stretching and focus on it. You might invite children to stretch and then to return slowly to normal posture, then to stretch again, perhaps reaching out a little bit farther than the time before.

Centering. "Slowly come back to your deepest inner self and get in touch with the love you feel for the whole planet. Let your heart feel itself opening to the whole world."

Theme. "Just about everyone has had a hero. I'll bet you've had a hero, too, someone you admired and tried to imitate, someone you dressed like and even talked like. In this meditation, Jesus promised that we will be witnesses to him all over the earth, that we will be signs of Christ."

Scripture. Read Acts 1:8.

Petition. "Let's ask Jesus for the gift to be a visible sign. Say words like, "Jesus, help me be a Christ-sign, so others will see you in me."

Meditation. (Music softly.) "See Jesus standing amid the disciples. He is their hero. And you are there too, feeling very proud of Jesus and wanting to do what you need to do. Hear Jesus telling you, among the disciples, that you will witness him to the ends of the earth. Listen as Jesus gives you permission to make him one of your heroes. Listen as he tells you to go all over the planet encouraging others to become signs of Christ, too. Picture yourself going somewhere and telling someone what you have seen and heard about Jesus. See what the music helps you to say to such a person." (Music up.)

Ending. Usual ending, being especially grateful for any indication of happiness in following Jesus.

Review. You might begin a discussion of the meditative experience by asking some evocative questions such as, "Where in the world would you like to travel to tell about Jesus?" "What things about Jesus would you tell first to people?" "Who among your family and friends might you like to take with you on a journey to talk about Jesus?"

4. JESUS DEPARTS

Music. Find some goodbye music that allows for a variety of feelings during leave-taking.

Relaxation. "Let yourself grow quiet so you can say goodbye to Jesus with your body as well as your mind. Breathe slowly from the pit of your stomach to build up your feelings of reverence."

Centering. "Focus on a balloon. Let it be whatever color you like. See how it feels to hold it so it won't float away."

Theme. "Everyone is gathered around Jesus, shaking his hand, touching him, and kissing him goodbye. See how he is ready to leave. During the meditation you will be able to tell him goodbye in any way you wish."

Scripture. Read Acts 1:9.

Petition. "Say to Jesus something like, 'Jesus, help me believe that you are returning to your Father to prepare a place for me in his kingdom.'"

Meditation. (Music softly.) "See, Jesus notices you in the crowd and he beckons you to come closer to him. Go near to him and tell him how much you love him and how much he loves you. Somehow, even though you feel sad to see him go, you realize that he must return to his Father. If you like, choose your favorite colored helium balloon and give Jesus the string to hold. Tell him he can remember you with that balloon. Then you can watch your balloon rise as Jesus departs. You may not be able to see Jesus but watch the balloon rising higher and higher in the sky, passing the clouds. And you will know Jesus is taking your balloon—which symbolizes your heart—with him to his Father. As the music plays, feel how you are connected to Jesus even when he leaves." (Music up.)

Ending. Usual ending.

Review. Begin by inviting children to talk about their balloon and, from that, move into an awareness of how they remain connected to the ascended Jesus. The affective responses of letting Jesus go and of still being connected are more important here than doctrinal or theological refinements. Focus in review on the affective relationship between the child and Jesus.

5. WAITING FOR JESUS' RETURN

Music. Floating, smooth pastoral music to accompany the rising and floating of many balloons.

Relaxation. "We are going to have balloons in our meditation again today, so in your imagination use your breath to fill up your balloon with air. Blow several deep breaths slowly into your imaginary balloon."

Centering. "Put your own heart, or self, into your balloon. Watch your heart inside your balloon."

Theme. "Jesus ascends to his Father, disappears for a time, but because he promises to return again one day we believe and look for the day when he will come again. We use our imaginary balloons to help us realize how it feels to be waiting for someone to return."

Scripture. Read Acts 1:10-11.

Petition. "Jesus, I believe you will return to me and I am waiting for you with an open heart."

Meditation. (Music softly.) "Imagine yourself standing in

the school yard with all your classmates (or in your yard with your friends), each one watching his or her colored balloon rising in the sky till it finally disappears. At first you can see a sky alive with floating rainbow colors. Eventually, the colors float out of sight, but because you know you have seen your balloon rise, you can believe it has gone somewhere unknown to you. But let yourself also believe that it will return again one day. You may not see it today or tomorrow, but you know one day it may come floating by and you will be happy to recognize it. It will be the same when Jesus returns. You will recognize him as surely as you would recognize your special balloon. As the music plays, let the balloons float out of sight, and then get in touch with being ready for your balloon's return." (Music up.)

Ending. Usual ending, adding, "Be sure to remind God that you know the color of your balloon and will recognize it when it returns."

Review. Here the emphasis will be on the children's awareness of waiting in readiness for the return of something special. Also, point out the collective nature of the experience: It is not only your balloon which rises and goes away, but everyone's, and therefore everyone is sharing a similar kind of waiting experience.

Note

It might be helpful to have children do drawings of their balloons. Some may wish to design a balloon in great detail, painting their name on it or decorating it in various colors to emphasize its uniqueness. Others may choose to draw a sky full of balloons. In any case, such drawings become mementos of the special ascension experience of Jesus, an experience, by the way, whose meaning and significance not many adults grasp.

CHAPTER **16**

Meditations on the Days
of Pentecost

1. GATHERED IN THE UPPER ROOM: WAITING

Music. Choose selections having a sense of mystery or expectancy, but not frighteningly so.

Relaxation. I suggest focusing on the breath, perhaps in the heart area.

Centering. "Slowly let yourself become aware how God is present to you in your heart and relax in the awareness that God loves you."

Theme. "Before Jesus ascended to his Father's heavenly kingdom, he promised his friends that he would send the Holy Spirit to them. In this meditation the apostles are in the upper room waiting for that promise to be fulfilled. You are a good friend of Jesus, so imagine yourself waiting in the upper room for the Spirit to come. As you enter into meditation, let some questions be in your mind: Who is the Holy Spirit? What does the Spirit look like? How would I recognize the Spirit? Jesus said the Spirit would fill you with love and special gifts. Let yourself wonder what gifts the Spirit will bring and how you will be filled with love. What does love feel like?"

Scripture. Acts 2:1.

Petition. "Let's ask Jesus for the gifts we need, saying, 'Jesus, prepare me for the unknown, for the mystery moments when your Spirit comes to me.' "

Meditation. (Music softly.) "Picture all the apostles and others in the upper room. Take a look around and see the faces of those waiting with you. Who are they? Notice how wide open their eyes are and how anxious they seem to be. Waiting for someone special to arrive is a very exciting feeling. Jesus is going to keep his promise to you. Be very still now as you wait in silence for the Spirit of God to come to you. Afterwards you can share with us what you experienced." (Music up.)

Ending. "Thank Jesus for sending his Spirit and for making known his Spirit to you."

Review. Ask children how they experienced the Spirit, how it felt, what it looked like. Especially ask what gifts the Spirit gave them and how they can use these gifts in their everyday lives.

2. THE SPIRIT ARRIVES: SIGNS OF THE SPIRIT

Music. Use music that evokes a sense of wind and fire and excitement.

Relaxation. Use a favorite method.

Centering. Use a familiar formula.

Theme. "In this meditation you are going to experience the moment the Holy Spirit appears to the apostles. Since you are there with them in the upper room, you will want to open your heart, your mind, and your body to receive the Spirit. Watch the Spirit touch each person in the room."

Scripture. Acts 2:2-3.

Petition. "Let's ask Jesus for a gift, saying, 'Jesus, open me, fill me, stay in me always.' "

Meditation. (Music softly.) "Imagine you are sitting very quietly with your friends waiting for the arrival of the

Spirit. Then you hear a loud noise. Listen! It's happening so quickly that everyone is shocked and surprised. You can hear a strong wind blowing, and the whole room is filled with the sound. Listen again; the sound continues. Now look above the heads of your friends and you begin to see something very unusual, very different. It looks like a bright flame of fire. Imagine you lift your hand over your own head and you realize the bright flame is over you too. Don't worry; this fire will not burn you or hurt you. It has magic powers, different from anything else you have ever known or seen before. This fire is a sign of the Holy Spirit who has come to you just as Jesus promised the Spirit would. Open yourself to the Spirit. Watch the Spirit enter your heart. Feel the Spirit touch you and let your whole being be filled with the presence and awareness of the Holy Spirit." (Music up.)

Ending. "Thank the Holy Spirit for coming into your heart and ask to know the gifts the Spirit has given you."

Review. Children enjoy wind and fire. Discuss their images of the Spirit and their feelings in reaction to the Spirit's touch.

3. SPEAKING OTHER LANGUAGES: THE GIFT OF TONGUES

Music. Find a selection that is joyful and bubbly, that reflects delight and wonder at creation.

Relaxation. Use a favorite method of the children.

Centering. "Be aware of God in your heart and let that awareness spread throughout your body. Let yourself feel God's presence, especially in your throat and mouth and tongue—in all the parts of you that help you speak."

Theme. "In this meditation you are still in the upper room with the apostles where the Spirit is giving special gifts. Today we will imagine the Spirit giving the gift of language. Have you ever spoken another language or heard someone speak in a way that was foreign to you? The Spirit is giving the apostles the gift of tongues so they can speak many languages and tell people from all over the world about the marvelous gifts of God."

Scripture. Acts 2:4.

Petition. "Ask Jesus for a special gift. Say, 'Jesus I believe you always keep your promise in the surprises you send us through your Spirit.' "

Meditation. (Music softly.) "Picture yourself still in the upper room with the disciples. Feel how the Spirit is making the Spirit known to you in the sound of the wind and in the flame of fire. Feel the Spirit's presence now within you and expect a great surprise. The Spirit is going to give special gifts now. Picture the apostles receiving the gift of tongues so they may speak in foreign languages to people from foreign lands. Picture yourself all of a sudden speaking another language to your friends without anyone ever teaching you. And they understand you! What a surprise! Enjoy this gift of the Spirit with the apostles." (Music up.)

Ending. "Thank God for the gift of knowing how it can feel to have the ability to speak other languages and tell of the wonders of God."

Review. Talk about foreign languages, the hundreds of different languages spoken throughout the world, and how important in telling people about Jesus it is to be able to speak different languages. Children may know relatives or friends who speak a foreign language. Let them tell stories about different languages.

4. SPEAKING TO THE PEOPLE: SHARING THE SPIRIT'S GIFTS

Music. Use music that creates a mood of excitement and of crowds of happy people.

Relaxation. Use a familiar method.

Centering. Use the method followed in meditation 3, or any familiar one.

Theme. "The apostles in the upper room are so high with excitement, wonder, surprise, and enthusiasm at the gift of languages they just received from the Spirit that they throw open the doors and run outside to tell the large group that has gathered about the wonderful experience just happening to them."

Scripture. Acts 2:5-8.

Petition. "Let's ask Jesus for a gift. Say, 'Jesus, continue to speak to me about the wonders of your Spirit.'"

Meditation. (Music softly.) "Imagine you are running down the steps from the upper room and throwing open the doors on a beautiful morning. Listen as the apostles begin to speak in more than fifteen different languages. See how wide the people's eyes and mouths open as they listen in amazement to the words of the apostles. Even though you can't understand all the words they speak, let yourself hear with your inside ears about the wonderful things God has done for you and others. He loves you so much." (Music up.)

Ending. "In the surprise and joy of your own heart talk to Jesus about the message his Spirit has shared with you."

Review. Ask children about the messages they heard the Spirit speaking through the mouths of the apostles. Were the messages for the whole world? Did the messages have a significance for the children themselves? How did it feel to hear in your imagination apostles speaking in many different languages?

5. PETER'S MESSAGE: WE HAVE ALL RECEIVED THE SPIRIT'S GIFTS

Music. Use selections of joy and love.

Relaxation. Use a familiar method.

Centering. "Jesus wants to reveal his wonderful gifts through you. Imagine yourself filled with the Spirit's love. Picture this love-color and feel its warmth in the deepest part of you."

Theme. "You don't have to speak many languages to tell about God. Using your own tongue and voice you can sing praises and shout out the joy of the Risen Lord. In earlier meditations, we waited for the Spirit, opened ourselves to receive the Spirit, and recognized the Spirit's presence in the wind and fire. We listened to the gift of tongues through the apostles and received the message of God's marvelous works in our own lives. Now we become aware that Jesus wants to reveal God's wonderful gifts through us."

Scripture. Acts 2:16-17.

Petition. "In a spirit of joy let's ask Jesus for a gift, saying, 'Jesus, your name is a song in my heart and a prayer on my lips.' "

Meditation. (Music softly.) "Let yourself feel your voice singing God's praise and shouting out joy for the Risen Lord. Picture yourself in your smile giving Jesus to others. Picture yourself giving and receiving a warm hug. Let the touch of Jesus be felt through your hug. Imagine in the beauty of your face the Spirit shining forth for others to see. See how fully alive you begin to feel in the radiance of the Spirit. Let yourself feel the special gifts the Spirit gives you, especially so that you can tell everyone by your smile and your hug and your beauty that Jesus lives today in your heart and in the world through you." (Music up.)

Ending. "Thank the Holy Spirit for coming into you and making you feel fully alive today."

Review. Talk about smiles and hugs and people who are attractive to be with. Ask the children about the Holy Spirit and the gifts they would like to receive from the Spirit.

CHAPTER **17**

Meditations on Mary, the Mother of Jesus

1. SAYING YES TO GOD: THE ANNUNCIATION

Music. Delicate, soft music that affirms the gift of life.

Relaxation. "Imagine you are surrounded by a cloud, a very loving cloud. As you let your body relax, the cloud will support you. Little by little, you can let go completely into being held and comforted by the cloud. With each breath, feel yourself settling down into the cloud just a little bit more." (Pause a bit for five or six slow breaths.)

Centering. "Now focus on yourself and how carefully held and protected you are. Enjoy being loved like that, for that is how it feels to be held by God."

Theme. "Have you ever received an announcement that something great was going to happen to you? Do you remember what it felt like? Remember who told you and what you said to the person? A message like this comes to Mary, telling her she is to be the mother of Jesus. She says 'Yes' to the message and that 'Yes' is very important to us because it brings us Jesus."

Scripture. Use Luke 1:26-38, but tell the story in your own words according to the age level of the children.

Petition. "Let's ask Jesus each in our own way to help us say 'Yes' with an open heart to whatever he asks of us today."

Meditation. (Music softly.) "Picture Mary near her house as she hears the angel's message that she would be the mother of the Savior. See how surprised she must be as the angel tells her she was chosen out of all the women of the world. See if you can sense how she feels about the message. You can tell that she doesn't understand completely what it means, but hear her say 'Yes' to the invitation because she trusts in God and really believes this is what God wants her to do. Imagine yourself being with Mary. As the music plays, talk to her in your own words and thank her for accepting this wonderful invitation." (Music up.)

Ending. "Take a moment to thank God for the privilege of being with Mary in your heart. Remember what you and Mary said and did together. And when you're ready, you may open your eyes and sit up."

Review. Elicit feeling responses when possible. Also ask the children to share what happened to them in interaction with Mary. Some may be attracted to the angelic appearance. Still others may respond best when they share the times they themselves received an important announcement.

2. SHARING A SECRET: THE VISITATION

Music. Find a pastoral selection that suggests movement, taking a happy walk.

Relaxation. Use some favorite method.

Centering. Use a familiar way.

Theme. "Today we are going to take a walk with Mary over the hills that lead to her cousin Elizabeth's house. Recall the last time you traveled to see someone you loved. Do you remember how you felt getting ready for the trip, before you arrived? Remember how the someone you loved was waiting for you? Did you share secrets when you got together? Mary and Elizabeth each had a secret to share, which brought joy to each other."

Scripture. Luke 1:39-56. Tell the story simply, in outline form, using your own words.

Petition. "Ask Jesus for a gift. Use words like, 'Jesus, help me find a way to bring an unexpected joy to someone's heart today.'"

Meditation. (Music softly.) "Imagine you are with Mary and you are approaching the door of Elizabeth's home. Hear Mary call Elizabeth's name. Watch Elizabeth come running out and the two women hug each other happily. Listen as Elizabeth tells Mary she is going to have a baby and listen to the excitement in Mary's voice as she tells Elizabeth she is going to have a baby too. See how happy they both are. See how big Elizabeth's smile is. Listen to what they say to each other as they share more details about their secrets, their new babies. Perhaps you can think of a happy secret about yourself that you would like to tell Mary and Elizabeth." (Music up.)

Ending. Follow some standard ending.

Review. Perhaps the joy of sharing secrets would be a good theme. You might begin by asking, "What person do you usually share your secrets with first?" Another theme to discuss with children is that of visiting. For example, ask, "Whom do you like to visit?" "Where do they live?" "When did you go there?" Friendship and sharing are at the heart of the gospel message.

3. BEARING A CHILD: JESUS IS BORN

Music. Joyful music, full of new life.

Relaxation. "How do babies relax? They yawn and they stretch. Let's do that. Let's stretch as far as we can, using arms and legs, then take a big yawn—which is a kind of inner stretching. Let's do stretching and yawning a few more times till we feel very relaxed."

Centering. "Be aware of God's life in you filling up all the relaxed places. If you still have a place in your body or mind that's not relaxed, stretch it so that God can fill it up with his presence."

Theme. "Today we're going to meditate on the birth of Jesus. Have you ever seen anything that is newly born? A baby brother or sister? A baby chick, yellow and fluffy? How soft and cuddly and small they are. Wherever it happens, brand new life makes us smile on the outside, and happy and excited on the inside. Mary and Joseph felt that way when Jesus was born. So did your mother and father the day you came into the world."

Scripture. Luke 1:1-7. The story is so familiar you probably won't need to read it aloud.

Petition. "For a gift from God, let's ask God to let us see and hear and feel what the baby Jesus must have been like."

Meditation. (Music softly.) "Begin by imagining the scene where Jesus was born. Go near the crib where he is resting as a tiny baby. Yes, Jesus was once a tiny baby who smiled and cried and laughed just like you. Go to the crib and peek in. You may touch him gently if you like. Notice the shape of his mouth, his nose, and his eyes. See him look at you. What color are his eyes? You can tell he feels very comfortable being with you. As the music plays, spend some time by the crib talking to Jesus with your heart." (Music up.)

Ending. "Use your own words to thank God for sending Jesus into our world, and thank Mary and Joseph for taking good care of him. When you're ready, you can sit up and share with us what happened to you."

Review. Focus on the infant Jesus. Ask what he looked like. Some may wish to draw a picture of Jesus. Children a bit older are capable of noticing more details than younger children. Evoke responses that relate to Mary as a mother, and ask for personal experiences of a caring mother (or someone who cares).

4. YOURSELF AS A GIFT: THE PRESENTATION

Music. Solemn, sacred music that reflects the atmosphere of a cathedral or church.

Relaxation. Follow some favorite method.

Centering. Use a usual procedure.

Theme. "When you were a child your parents brought you to church to be baptized, to be presented to God. Did someone ever tell you what you wore that day? Did they tell you who held you? Today, we're going to watch Mary and Joseph in our imaginations as they bring their child Jesus to the temple to offer him to God."

Scripture. Luke 2:22-38. You may want to tell the essence of the story in your own words.

Petition. "Let's all ask Jesus for a gift by saying in our own way, 'Jesus, continue to fill me with the life and love of your spirit.' "

Meditation. (Music softly.) "Go with Mary and Joseph to the temple. See, they are carrying their baby and bringing him to where the priest is standing. Watch them hold out the baby to the priest who will bless him. Perhaps you can go up to Mary and Joseph. Tell them what a pretty baby they have, and tell them how your parents offered you to God like that when you were a baby. Tell them how you were baptized. Explain how that means you were filled with God's life and spirit of love. Tell Mary and Joseph about yourself now and how much the grace of God has grown in you since then." (Music up.)

Ending. Use a standard ending.

Review. Let the children talk about baptism, what it means, how it happens, and where it happens. Ask them what they told Mary and Joseph about themselves.

5. Getting Lost, Then Found: The Finding in the Temple

Music. Find a selection that has the hint of anxiety and searching, perhaps confusion too.

Relaxation. Use a standard procedure.

Centering. Use a standard procedure.

Theme. "Today's theme is about being lost—really lost—then being found again. Have you ever been lost? How old were you when it happened? How long were you by yourself? How happy and safe did it feel when you were found, when you were reunited once again with someone you knew and loved? Jesus had an experience of being lost, too."

Scripture. Luke 2:41-52. Tell the story simply, in your own way.

Petition. "Ask Jesus in your own way for a gift you need for your heart. Say, 'Jesus, help me to find you whenever I get lost.'"

Meditation. "Jesus is twelve years old and he is lost. Imagine his mother and father looking all over the big temple for him. See hundreds of rooms and courtyards, doors and chambers. Jesus could be behind any one of them. What if he is also wandering around looking for them? They could keep passing one another again and again. Feel how anxious and frightened they are when they can't find Jesus. Three days go by before they find him! Join Jesus, Mary, and Joseph when they are finally reunited. Share their joy at being together again. Tell them how it felt when you were lost. As the music plays, talk to Jesus and see if being lost feels the same for him as it does for you." (Music up.)

Ending. Use standard procedure.

Review. Invite children to talk about times when they were lost and how it felt. Help them to get a sense that they share the being-lost-then-found experience with

Jesus. Let them feel moments of his humanity and identify with them. Perhaps children may want to talk about ways they can get lost.

Note

By now, the structure of a contemplation is quite familiar to you. You notice how each gospel episode can be viewed from the child's perspective. You see how a contemplation is most effective when it has a single point, a simple focus.

As you devise new and different contemplations for your children, use the step-by-step formula I have suggested throughout Part III. Whenever you can connect a gospel story to a typical event in a child's life, you can be sure that the contemplation of it will prove fruitful.

I hope you will try designing your own contemplations. It really is fun. It's meaningful if you invite the children to help you create their meditations. Besides, if you develop meditations with the children, you will build up in them confidence to design their own meditations in the future. Thus, you will have generated a self-directed contemplative child—one who is aware of *Our Treasured Heritage* as a Christian. What a gift to the world!